BASIC

English
Grammar

FOURTH EDITION
WORKBOOK

VOLUME B

Betty S. Azar
Stacy A. Hagen

Basic English Grammar, Fourth Edition
Workbook Volume B

Azar Associates: Shelley Hartle, Editor, and Sue Van Etten, Manager

Pearson Education, 10 Bank Street, White Plains, NY 10606

Staff credits: The people who made up the *Basic English
Grammar, Fourth Edition, Workbook Volume B* team,
representing editorial, production, design, and manufacturing, are
Dave Dickey, Nancy Flaggman, Amy McCormick, Robert Ruvo,
and Marian Wassner.

Text composition: S4Carlisle Publishing Services

Illustrations: Don Martinetti and Chris Pavely

Printed in the United States of America

ISBN 10: 0-13-294225-9
ISBN 13: 978-0-13-294225-6

2 17

For Julianna

-S. H.

Contents

The titles listed below, for example, *Singular pronouns* + *be*, refer to section names, not practice titles. In general, one section has multiple exercises.
The chart numbers refer to the grammar explanations in the *Basic English Grammar* **Student Book**.

Preface

The *Basic English Grammar Workbook* is a self-study textbook. It is keyed to the explanatory grammar charts found in *Basic English Grammar, Fourth Edition,* a classroom teaching text for English language learners. Students can use the *Workbook* independently to enhance their understanding of English structures. Practice ranges from the basic to the more challenging so students can choose from a variety of exercises that will help them use English meaningfully and correctly.

This *Workbook* is also a resource for teachers who need exercise material for additional classwork, homework, testing, or individualized instruction.

The answers to the practices can be found in the *Answer Key* in the back of the *Workbook.* Its pages are perforated so that they can be detached to make a separate booklet. However, if teachers want to use the *Workbook* as a classroom teaching text, the *Answer Key* can be removed at the beginning of the term.

Chapter 9
Expressing Past Time, Part 2

▶ **Practice 1. Where, when, what time, why.** (Chart 9-1)
Make simple past questions and answers. Use **Where . . . go?**, **When/What time . . . leave?**,
Why . . . go there? and the given information.

> Oscar's travel plans
>
> To Mexico City
> Leave on March 22
> To visit family

> Serena's travel plans
>
> the Canary Islands
> Leave at 6 AM
> For vacation

Oscar's plans

1. A: _____Where did Oscar go?_____

   B: _____He went to Mexico City._____

2. A: _____

   B: _____

3. A: _____

   B: _____

Serena's plans

4. A: _____

   B: _____

5. A: _____

   B: _____

6. A: _____

   B: _____

▶ **Practice 2. *Where, when, what time, why.*** (Chart 9-1)
Write the letter of the correct response next to the question.

1. Who did you invite to your party? ___*b*___   a. A new TV.

2. When did your plane arrive? _____   ✓ b. My best friends.

3. Why did you eat two breakfasts? _____   c. In 2003.

4. When did you travel to Peru? _____   d. In Toronto.

5. Where did you live during high school? _____   e. Because I was very hungry.

6. What did you buy? _____   f. A few minutes ago.

▶ **Practice 3. *Where, when, what time, why.*** (Chart 9-1)
Make questions for the given answers.

1. A: _____*Where did you study last night?*_____

   B: At the library. (I studied at the library last night.)

2. A: _____

   B: At 10:00. (I left the library at 10:00.)

3. A: _____

   B: Because it closed at 10:00. (I left because the library closed at 10:00.)

4. A: _____

   B: To the park. (My friends and I went to the park yesterday afternoon.)

5. A: _____

   B: Two days ago. (Sandra got back from Brazil two days ago.)

6. A: _____

   B: Because he was sick. (Bobby was in bed because he was sick.)

7. A: _____

   B: Because he didn't get enough sleep. (Bobby was sick because he didn't get enough sleep.)

8. A: _____

   B: Online. (I bought my sandals online.)

sandals

▶ **Practice 4. *Why didn't.*** (Chart 9-1)
Make questions. Begin with ***Why didn't***.

1. A: I looked for you at the meeting, but you didn't come.   *Why didn't you come?*
   B: Because I had to work overtime.

2. A: You needed help, but you didn't ask the teacher. _____
   B: Because no one else had questions, and I felt stupid.

3. A: The homework is due today, and you didn't bring it. _____
   B: Because I fell asleep while I was studying last night.

4. A: You told a lie. You didn't tell me the truth. _____
   B: Because I was afraid of your reaction.

5. A: Sharon looked sad. You didn't go to her party. _____
   B: Because I forgot it was her birthday.

6. A: Look at this mess! You didn't clean your bedroom. _____
   B: Because I was too tired.

▶ **Practice 5. *What* + verb review.** (Chart 9-2)
Make questions. Pay attention to verb tenses.

1. A: ___*What did you buy?*___
   B: A digital camera. (We bought a digital camera.)

2. A: ___*Did you buy a digital camera?*___
   B: Yes, we did. (We bought a digital camera.)

3. A: _____
   B: Math. (I studied math.)

4. A: _____
   B: Yes, I did. (I studied math.)

5. A: _____
   B: A map. (They're looking at a map.)

6. A: _____
   B: Yes, they are. (They're looking at a map.)

7. A: _____
   B: English grammar. (I dreamed about English grammar last night.)

8. A: _____
   B: Yes, she is. (She's a new employee.)

9. A: _____

    B: Algebra. (She tutors algebra.)

10. A: _____

    B: His country. (David talked about his country.)

11. A: _____

    B: Yes, he did. (David talked about his country.)

12. A: _____

    B: Nothing in particular. (I'm thinking about nothing in particular.)

13. A: _____

    B: Nothing special. (*Nothing in particular* means "nothing special.")

14. A: _____

    B: Spiders. (I am afraid of spiders.)

a spider

▶ **Practice 6. Understanding questions with *who*.** (Chart 9-3)
Write questions and short answers for the given sentences.

1. Julie called the police.

    a. Who called _____*the police?*_____ Julie.

    b. Who did _____*Julie call?*_____ The police.

2. The nurse checked Lea.

    a. Who checked _____ The nurse.

    b. Who did _____ Lea.

3. Felix helped the new assistant.

    a. Who did _____ The new assistant.

    b. Who helped _____ _____

4. Professor Jones taught the advanced students.

    a. Who taught _____ Professor Jones.

    b. Who did _____ _____

5. The police caught the thief.

   a. Who did _____ _____

   b. Who caught _____ _____

6. Tommy dreamed about a monster.

   a. Who dreamed about _____ _____

   b. Who did _____ _____

▶ **Practice 7. Using *who*.** (Chart 9-3)
Make questions with ***who***.

1. Ron helped Judy.

   a. _____*Who helped Judy?*_____ Ron.

   b. _____*Who did Ron help?*_____ Judy.

2. The doctor examined the patient.

   a. _____ The patient.

   b. _____ The doctor.

3. Miriam called the supervisor.

   a. _____ Miriam.

   b. _____ The supervisor.

4. The students surprised the teacher.

   a. _____ The students.

   b. _____ The teacher.

5. Andrew and Catherine waited for Mrs. Allen.

   a. _____ Mrs. Allen.

   b. _____ Andrew and Catherine.

► **Practice 8. Using *who*.** (Chart 9-3)
There were some parties last week. Write questions and answers using the words from the box.

Questions: Who had a ____ party?
            Who did ____ invite?

Host*	Party	Guests
Mrs. Adams	birthday party for her son	her son's friends
Dr. Martin	New Year's party	her employees
Professor Brown	graduation party	his students

1. _____Who had a birthday party?_____   Mrs. Adams.

2. _____Who did Mrs. Adams invite?_____   Her son's friends.

3. _____   Professor Brown.

4. _____   His students.

5. _____   Dr. Martin.

6. _____   Her employees.

► **Practice 9. Using *who*.** (Chart 9-3)
Make questions with ***who***.

1. A: _____Who did you see?_____
   B: Ken. (I saw Ken.)

2. A: _____
   B: Ken. (I talked to Ken.)

3. A: _____
   B: Nancy. (I visited Nancy.)

4. A: _____
   B: Ahmed. (Ahmed answered the question.)

5. A: _____
   B: Mr. Lee. (Mr. Lee taught the English class.)

*host = the person who gives a party.

6. A: _____

    B: Carlos. (Carlos helped me.)

7. A: _____

    B. Gina. (I helped Gina.)

8. A: _____

    B: My brother. (My brother carried the suitcases.)

9. A: _____

    B: Yuko. (Yuko called.)

▶ **Practice 10. Irregular verbs: Group 5.** (Chart 9-4)
Check (✓) the sentences that are true for you. Write the present form for each verb in *italics*.

                                                       Present Form

1. _____ I *forgot* to do my homework last week.   ____*forget*____

2. _____ My teacher *gave* me extra work last week.   _____

3. _____ I *understood* my teacher on the first day of class.   _____

4. _____ I *hurt* my back last year.   _____

5. _____ I *spent* money on snack food yesterday.   _____

6. _____ I *shut* a window last night.   _____

7. _____ I *lent* some money to a friend last year.   _____

8. _____ I *cut* something with a sharp knife yesterday.   _____

9. _____ I once *hit* my finger with a hammer.   _____

10. _____ I *made* only one mistake on my last grammar test.   _____

11. _____ Ice-cream cones *cost* a lot when I was a child.   _____

an ice-cream cone

▶ **Practice 11. Irregular verbs: Group 5.** (Chart 9-4)
Complete each sentence on the next page with the simple past form of a verb from the box.
In some sentences, more than one verb is correct. The number in parentheses tells you how
many verbs you can use.

cost	forget	hit	lend	✓ shut	understand
cut	give	hurt	make	spend	

Jonathan had a bad day yesterday.

1. He woke up early because a dog was barking outside. He _____*shut*_____ his bedroom window too hard and cracked the glass. (1)

2. He _____ to bring his homework to class. His teacher wasn't happy. (1)

3. He _____ a lot of mistakes on his math quiz. (1)

4. His teacher _____ him a low grade on his research paper. (1)

5. He thought he _____ the research assignment, but his teacher said he did it wrong. (1)

6. He broke a glass container in chemistry class. When he picked up the glass, he _____ his hand. (2)

7. He left his lunch at home, so he bought food in the cafeteria. It _____ a lot. He had no money left. (1)

8. Because he _____ all his money, he had no money for the bus. (1)

9. A friend _____ him some bus money, but he lost it. (2)

10. During lunch, he played soccer with his friends. Someone kicked the ball, and it _____ him in the face. (2)

11. He couldn't open his eye, and his face _____ the rest of the day. (1)

▶ **Practice 12. Irregular verbs: Group 6.** (Chart 9-5)
Check (✓) the sentences that are true for you. Write the present form for each verb in *italics*.

		Present Form
1.	_____ I *knew* all the answers in the last exercise.	_____*know*_____
2.	_____ I *felt* happy all day yesterday.	_____
3.	_____ When I was a child, I *kept* animals for pets.	_____
4.	_____ I *swam* in a pool last month.	_____
5.	_____ I *threw* away some homework yesterday.	_____
6.	_____ I *drew* pictures in my grammar book yesterday.	_____
7.	_____ I *grew* vegetables last summer.	_____

8. _____ I often *fell* down when I was a child.   _____

9. _____ I *won* a prize when I was a child.   _____

10. _____ I *blew* bubbles with bubblegum yesterday.   _____

bubblegum

▶ **Practice 13. Irregular verbs: Group 6.** (Chart 9-5)
Complete each sentence with the simple past form of a verb from the box. There is only one correct verb for each sentence.

✓ blow	fall	grow	know	throw
draw	feel	keep	swim	won

A crazy day in the classroom

1. Every time the teacher spoke, she _____ *blew* _____ a whistle.

2. Some students _____ funny pictures on the ceiling.

3. It was a hot, sunny day. Snow _____ outside the classroom.

4. The students _____ happy when they heard there was a test.
   They cheered.

5. The teacher didn't want her lesson plans. She _____ them in the
   garbage can.

6. Flowers _____ on the teacher's desk. They smelled wonderful.

7. One student _____ a pet mouse in a box on her desk.

8. A goldfish _____ upside down in the fish bowl.

9. The class played a game. The teacher asked questions, but no one _____ the answers.

10. Both teams _____ a prize.

▶ **Practice 14. Irregular verbs: Group 7.** (Chart 9-6)
Check (✓) the sentences that are true for you. Write the present form for each verb in *italics*.

                                                                    Present Form

1. _____ I once *held* a big spider in my hand.   _____*hold*_____

2. _____ I once *bent* an iron bar.   _____

3. _____ I *shook* the hand of a famous person once.   _____

4. _____ I *became* friends with a famous person.   _____

5. _____ I *fed* a pet (dog, cat, fish, etc.) last week.   _____

6. _____ When I was a baby, I *bit* people.   _____

7. _____ I once *hid* some keys and later couldn't find them.   _____

8. _____ I sometimes *fought* with my friends when I was young.   _____

9. _____ When I was a child, I *built* sand castles at the beach. _____

a sand castle

► **Practice 15. Irregular verbs: Group 7.** (Chart 9-6)
Complete each sentence with the simple past form of a verb from the box. In some sentences, more than one verb fits. The number in parentheses tells you how many verbs you can use.

become	bite	feed	hide	shake
bend	✓ build	fight	held	

Puppy trouble

Thomas got a new puppy. He's having trouble with her. Here's what happened last week.

1. He _____*built*_____ a dog house for her, but she didn't want to sleep outdoors.
   She wanted to be inside. (1)

2. She likes to play in the rain. Yesterday, she got all wet. Then she came inside and
   _____ her tail. She got Thomas all wet. (1)

3. Thomas _____ her dog food, but she didn't eat it. She only wanted
   meat. (1)

4. He gave her dog toys, but she _____ the toys. He can't find them. (1)

5. The puppy likes to play with people. On Monday, she got excited and
   _____ the mail carrier's pant leg. Fortunately, her teeth didn't touch
   the skin. (3)

6. The mail carrier didn't understand and _____ upset. (1)

7. Thomas's big cat, Snow, doesn't like the puppy. Snow jumps at her and tries to scratch
   her. All last week, they _____. (1)

8. Thomas didn't want the puppy to get hurt. He _____ her in his arms a
   lot. (1)

9. The puppy likes to chew. She chewed Thomas's glasses.
   She _____ the frames, and now they are
   crooked. (2)

► **Practice 16. Complete and incomplete sentences.**
         (Chart 9-7)
Write the phrases or sentences in the correct column on the next page. Add capitalization and punctuation where necessary.

✓ we slept	before school starts
✓ at the store	before school starts, I help the teacher
they left	we ate at a restaurant
after they left	after we finish dinner
after several minutes	we were at home

Incomplete sentence	Complete sentence
at the store	*We slept.*

▶ **Practice 17. *After.*** (Chart 9-7)
Look at the pairs of sentences. Decide which action happened first and which action happened second. Then write sentences with ***after***. Pay special attention to the punctuation.

1. __*1*__ My computer crashed.

   __*2*__ I lost my information.

   After my computer crashed, I lost my information. ____ OR

   I lost my information after my computer crashed. ____

2. _____ I closed the freezer door.

   _____ I looked in the freezer.

   _____ OR

   _____

3. _____ I stood on the scale.

   _____ The nurse wrote down my weight.

   _____ OR

   _____

4. _____ I exercised.

_____ I put on my exercise clothes.

_____ OR

_____

5. _____ The alarm rang at the fire station.

_____ The firefighters got in their truck.

_____ OR

_____

▶ **Practice 18. *Before* and *after*.** (Chart 9-7)
Look at the pairs of sentences. Decide which action happened first and which action happened second. Then choose the two sentences that have the same meaning.

1. __*1*__ Joan washed the dishes.

__*2*__ Joan dried the dishes.

(a.) After Joan washed the dishes, she dried them.

b. Before Joan washed the dishes, she dried them.

c. After Joan dried the dishes, she washed them.

(d.) Before Joan dried the dishes, she washed them.

2. _____ It rained.

_____ The rain clouds came.

a. After it rained, the rain clouds came.

b. Before it rained, the rain clouds came.

c. After the rain clouds came, it rained.

d. Before the rain clouds came, it rained.

3. _____ Luis drove away.

_____ Luis started the car.

a. Before Luis drove away, he started the car.

b. Before Luis started the car, he drove away.

c. After Luis drove away, he started the car.

d. After Luis started the car, he drove away.

4. _____ I opened my eyes.

_____ I looked around the room.

    a. Before I opened my eyes, I looked around the room.

    b. After I opened my eyes, I looked around the room.

    c. Before I looked around the room, I opened my eyes.

    d. After I looked around the room, I opened my eyes.

▶ **Practice 19. *When* in questions and time clauses.** (Chart 9-8)
In each of the following pairs, one is a question and one is a time clause. Add the necessary punctuation: question mark or a comma.

1. a. When you called**,**
    b. When did you call**?**

2. a. When did the movie start
    b. When the movie started

3. a. When you were in high school
    b. When were you in high school

4. a. When it snowed
    b. When did it snow

5. a. When was Dave sick
    b. When Dave was sick

▶ **Practice 20. *When* in questions and time clauses.** (Chart 9-8)
Add punctuation: a question mark or a comma. Then make each time clause a complete sentence by adding another clause from the box.

> we felt sad.
> everyone clapped.
> ✓ I met them at the airport.
> we were happy to see you.
> the class had a test.

1. When was the Smiths' party**?**

2. When the Browns came**,** *I met them at the airport.*

3. When did you hear the good news

4. When Mr. King died

5. When were you here

6. When did we meet

7. When you arrived

8. When Kevin was absent

9. When the TV show ended

10. When was Mrs. Allen a teacher

▶ **Practice 21. *When* in questions and time clauses.** (Chart 9-8)
Use the given words to make (a) a simple past question and (b) a simple past clause. Then use your own words to complete the sentence in (b).

1. when \ rain \ it

    a. _____ *When did it rain?* _____

    b. _____ *When it rained, I went inside.* _____

2. when \ get sick \ you

    a. _____

    b. _____

3. when \ begin \ the problem

    a. _____

    b. _____

4. when \ visit \ they

    a. _____

    b. _____

▶ **Practice 22. Forms of the past progressive.** (Chart 9-9)
Create your own chart by completing the sentences with *study* and the correct form of the past progressive.

1. I _____ *was studying.* _____
2. You _____
3. He _____
4. She _____
5. Ray and I _____
6. Several students _____

7. We (not) _____
8. My children (not) _____
9. Dr. Roberts (not) _____
10. My friends and I (not) _____
11. Your friends (not) _____
12. I (not) _____

► **Practice 23. Forms of the present and past progressive.** (Chart 9-9)
Complete the sentences. Use a form of *be* + *sit*.

1. I _____ *am sitting* _____ in class right now.

2. I _____ *was sitting* _____ in class yesterday too.

3. You _____ in class right now.

4. You _____ in class yesterday too.

5. Tony _____ in class right now.

6. He _____ in class yesterday too.

7. We _____ in class today.

8. We _____ in class yesterday too.

9. Rita _____ in class now.

10. She _____ in class yesterday too.

11. Rita and Tony _____ in class today.

12. They _____ in class yesterday too.

► **Practice 24. *While* + past progressive.** (Chart 9-10)
Combine the sentences in each pair and add the correct punctuation. Use *while*.

1. We felt an earthquake.
   We were sitting in our living room last night.

   a. _____ *We felt an earthquake while we were sitting in our living room last night.* _____

   b. _____ *While we were sitting in our living room last night, we felt an earthquake.* _____

2. I was talking to the teacher yesterday.
   Another student interrupted me.

   a. _____

   b. _____

3. A police officer stopped another driver for speeding.
   We were driving to work.

   a. _____

   b. _____

4. I was walking in the forest.
   A dead tree fell over.

   a. _____

   b. _____

5. I was planting flowers in the garden.
   My dog began to bark at a squirrel.

   a. _____

   b. _____

a squirrel

▶ **Practice 25. *While* + past progressive.** (Chart 9-10)
Complete each sentence with the correct form of the verb.

While Tom (*drive*) _____*was driving*_____ down the road yesterday, his cell phone
                              1

(*ring*) _____. He (*answer, not*) _____ it because he
            2   3

(*want*) _____ to be careful. He (*notice*) _____ many drivers with
              4   5

cell phones. While he (*slow*) _____ down to make a turn, the driver
                                          6

in front of him suddenly (*drive*) _____ off the road into a ditch. Tom (*see*)
                                              7

_____ a cell phone in her hand.
       8

▶ **Practice 26. *While* + past progressive.** (Chart 9-10)
Complete each sentence with the correct form of the verb in parentheses.

A: My husband and I (*be*) _____*were*_____ at my cousin's last night. While we (*sit*)
   1
   _____ outside in the garden after dinner, her cat (*come*)
                    2
   _____ up to us with a snake in its mouth. I (*scream*) _____.
        3   4
B: What (*your cousin, do*) _____?
                                        5
A: She (*yell*) _____.
                    6
B: (*your husband, do*) _____ something?
                              7
A: He (*run*) _____ to the house. While he (*run*) _____,
                    8   9
   the cat (*run*) _____ after him. It was so funny. My cousin and I
                        10
   (*begin*) _____ to laugh until tears ran down our faces.
                  11

▶ **Practice 27. Simple past vs. past progressive.** (Chart 9-11)
Complete each sentence with the correct form of the verb in parentheses.

1. My roommate came home late last night. I (*sleep*) _____*was sleeping*_____ when
   she (*get*) _____ home.

2. When Gina (*call*) _____ last night, I (*take*) _____ a
   bubble bath.

3. I (*eat*) _____ lunch with my brother when I suddenly (*remember*)
   _____ my promise to pick my cousin up at school.

4. When the president (*begin*) _____ to speak, everyone (*become*)
   _____ quiet.

5. While I (*drive*) _____ to the airport, I (*see*) _____ an
   accident.

6. While Joan (*exercise*) _____, a salesperson (*come*)
   _____ to the door.

7. Pete (*send*) _____ a text message while his teacher (*talk*)
   _____. She (*tell*) _____ him to put his phone away.

8. When Albert (*hear*) _____ the police siren, he (*stop*)
   _____ on the side of the road.

▶ **Practice 28. Using *while* and *when*.** (Chart 9-11)
Read the story. Complete the sentences with information from the story.

A Nonstop Talker

While I was riding the train, a man sat down next to me. I was reading a book, and he asked me about it. I didn't want to talk. I just wanted to read my book, so I tried to answer quickly. While I was trying to finish, he interrupted me. He told me about his job, his boss, and his family. When I looked away, he continued to talk. When I looked at my watch, he continued to talk. Finally, I told him I wasn't feeling well. He began to tell me about his health. While he was giving me details about his doctor visits, I stood up. I excused myself and walked to the back of the train. When I looked ten minutes later, he was talking to another passenger. I'm sure he is talking to someone right now!

1. While the woman was reading a book, _____

2. When she answered the man's question, _____

3. When she looked away, _____

4. When she told him she wasn't feeling well, _____

5. While he was talking about doctors, _____

6. When she looked at him later, _____

▶ **Practice 29. Question review.** (Chapter 9)
Make questions. Use any appropriate question word: ***where, when, what time, why, who,*** or ***what.***

1. A: _____*Where did Simone go?*_____
   B: To a conference. (Simone went to a conference.)

2. A: _____
   B: Last month. (Simone went to a conference last month.)

3. A: _____
   B: Simone. (Simone went to a conference last month.)

4. A: _____
   B: Ali. (I saw Ali.)

5. A: _____
   B: At the train station. (I saw Ali at the train station.)

6. A: _____
   B: At 10:00. (I saw Ali at the train station at 10:00.)

7. A: _____

   B: Grammar. (The teacher is talking about grammar.)

8. A: _____

   B: Because the weather was hot. (The kids played in the pool because the weather was hot.)

9. A: _____

   B: The doctor's office. (The doctor's office called.)

10. A: _____

    B: Yesterday afternoon. (They called yesterday afternoon.)

11. A: _____

    B: The nurse. (I talked to the nurse.)

12. A: _____

    B: At home. (I was at home last night.)

13. A: _____

    B: "Very old." (*Ancient* means "very old.")

14. A: _____

    B: In an apartment. (I live in an apartment.)

15. A: _____

    B: A frog. (Annie has a frog in her pocket.)

▶ **Practice 30. Question review.** (Chapter 9)
Make questions for the given answers.

1. A: *When did you get up this morning? / What time do we need to leave? / Etc.*
   B: At 7:00.

2. A: _____
   B: In an apartment.

3. A: _____
   B: Yesterday.

4. A: _____
   B: It means "very, very good."

5. A: _____
   B: At 7:30.

6. A: _____
   B: A shirt.

7. A: _____
   B: My professor.

8. A: _____
   B: No, I didn't.

9. A: _____
   B: Because I wanted to.

10. A: _____
    B: Chemistry.

11. A: _____
    B: Yes, I did.

12. A: _____
    B: Nothing.

13. A: _____
    B: In the dormitory.

14. A: _____
    B: Because I was tired.

15. A: _____
    B: Last night.

▶ **Practice 31. Review: irregular verbs.** (Chapters 8 and 9)
Choose a sentence from the box that best completes each idea.

It sold in three days.   He ate too much for lunch.
Someone stole his wallet.   I caught a taxi.
She hung up after midnight.   She caught a cold yesterday.
✓ He said they were too noisy.   Sam bent over and picked it up for her.
It tore when she played outside.   I grew up there.
Several students came to class without   She found it on the teacher's desk.
their homework.

1. The teacher told the students to work more quietly. ___*He said they were too noisy.*___

2. Laurie doesn't feel good. _____

3. Beth lost her grammar book. _____

4. Jack had no money. _____

5. Peter didn't want dinner. _____

6. Susan didn't want to sell her car, but she needed money. _____

_____

7. Maria wore her best dress to school. _____

_____

8. Shelley's phone conversation began at 9:00 P.M. _____

_____

9. Kathy dropped her pen on the floor. _____

_____

10. I missed the bus for the airport yesterday. _____

11. The teacher was unhappy. _____

12. My hometown is Ames, Iowa. _____

▶ **Practice 32. Review: irregular verbs.** (Chapters 8 and 9)
Complete the sentences. Use the simple past form of the verbs from the box.

break	fall	lose	meet	steal	✓ throw
cost	know	make	spend	tell	wear

1. The baseball player _____*threw*_____ the ball to the catcher.

2. Rick _____ his arm when he fell on the ice.

3. Maggie didn't tell a lie. She _____ the truth.

4. We _____ a lot of money at the restaurant last night. The food was
good but expensive.

5. I wrote a check yesterday. I _____ a mistake on the check, so I tore it
up and wrote another one.

6. I _____ my winter jacket yesterday because the weather was cold.

7. Tom bought a new tie. It _____ a lot because it was a hand-painted
silk tie.

8. Leo read the story easily. The words in the story weren't new for him. He
_____ the vocabulary in the story.

9. I know Amanda Clark. I _____ her at a party a couple of weeks ago.

10. I dropped my book. It _____ to the floor.

11. Jack couldn't get into his apartment because he _____ his keys.

12. Someone _____ my bicycle, so I called the police.

▶ **Practice 33. Review: irregular verbs.** (Chapters 8 and 9)
Complete the sentences. Use the simple past form of the verbs from the box.

✓ begin	feed	fly	put	sing
build	fight	leave	shake	win

1. We were late for the graduation ceremony. It _____*began*_____ at 7:00, but we didn't get there until 7:15.

2. We _____ songs at the party last night and had a good time.

3. I _____ to Chicago last week. The plane was only five minutes late.

4. My plane _____ at 6:03 and arrived at 8:45.

5. We played a soccer game yesterday. The other team _____. We lost.

6. When I asked Dennis a question, he _____ his head no.

7. My daughter _____ a table in her woodworking class in high school.

8. Mike stole a spoon from the restaurant. He _____ it in his pocket before he walked out of the restaurant.

9. The two children wanted the same toy. They _____ for a few minutes. Then they decided to share it.

10. The baby was crying, so I _____ her some milk.

▶ **Practice 34. Verb review.** (Chapters 8 and 9)
Complete the sentences with the words in parentheses.

Part I.

Yesterday Fish (be) _____ in the river. He
                              1
(see) _____ Bear on the bank of the river. Here is
            2
their conversation.

BEAR: Good morning, Fish.

FISH: Good morning, Bear. How (you, be) _____ today?
                                                            3

BEAR: I (do) _____ fine, thank you. And you?
                          4

FISH: Fine, thanks.

BEAR: (you, would like) _____ to get out of the river and
                                              5
        (sit) _____ with me? I (need) _____ someone to talk to.
                      6   7

FISH: I (need, not) _____ to get out of the river for us to talk. We
                                    8
        can talk just the way we are now.

BEAR: Hmm.

FISH: Wait! What (you, do)

        _____?
                    9

BEAR: I (get) _____ in the river to join you.
                          10

FISH: Stop! This (be) _____ my river! I (trust, not) _____ you.
                                    11   12
        What (you, want) _____?
                                    13

BEAR: Nothing. Just a little conversation. I (want) _____ to tell you about my
                                                                    14
        problems. I (have) _____ a bad day yesterday.
                                15

FISH: Oh? What happened?

Part II.

BEAR: While I was walking through the woods,

        I (see) _____ a beehive. I (love)
                      16
        _____ honey. So I (stop)
              17
        _____. When I (reach)
                    18
        _____ inside the beehive
                19
        to get some honey, a great big bee

(come) _____ up behind me and stung* my ear. The sting (be)
                20

_____ very painful.
          21

FISH: I (believe, not) _____ you. Bees can't hurt bears. I
                                    22

(believe, not) _____ your story about a great big bee. All bees (be)
                          23

_____ the same size, and they (be, not) _____ big.
          24   25

BEAR: But it is true! Here. Come a little closer and look at my ear. I'll show you where the

big bee stung it.

FISH: Okay. Where (it, be) _____? Where (the bee, sting)
                                    26

_____ you?
            27

BEAR: Right here. See?

FISH: Stop! What (you, do) _____? Let go of me! Why (you, hold)
                                          28

_____ me?
              29

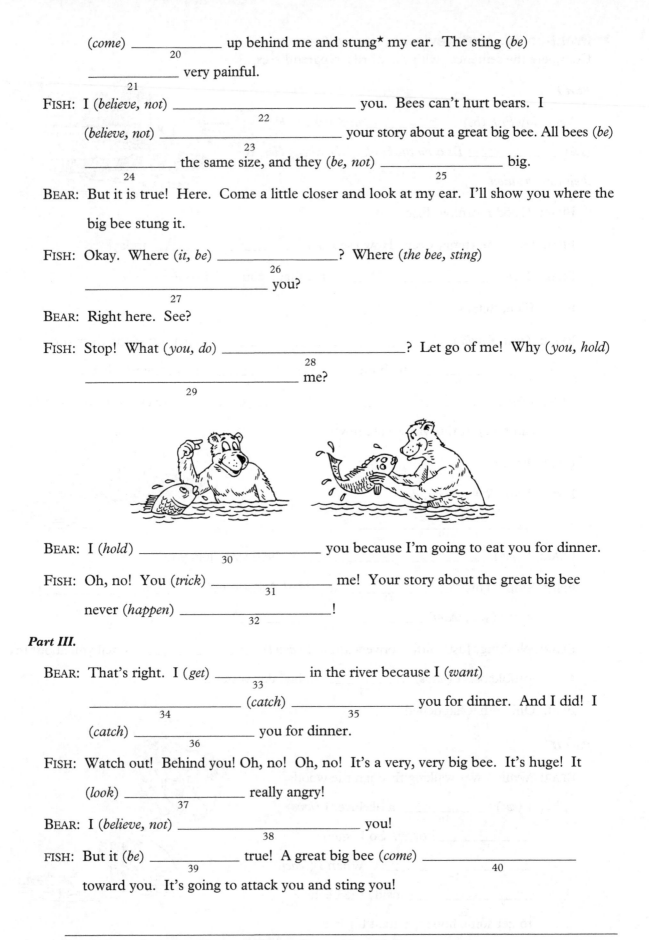

BEAR: I (hold) _____ you because I'm going to eat you for dinner.
                          30

FISH: Oh, no! You (trick) _____ me! Your story about the great big bee
                                    31

never (happen) _____!
                        32

Part III.

BEAR: That's right. I (get) _____ in the river because I (want)
                                    33

_____ (catch) _____ you for dinner. And I did! I
            34   35

(catch) _____ you for dinner.
                  36

FISH: Watch out! Behind you! Oh, no! Oh, no! It's a very, very big bee. It's huge! It

(look) _____ really angry!
              37

BEAR: I (believe, not) _____ you!
                              38

FISH: But it (be) _____ true! A great big bee (come) _____
                      39   40

toward you. It's going to attack you and sting you!

_____

*Stung is the past form of the verb sting, which means "to cause sharp pain."

BEAR: What? Where? I (*see, not*)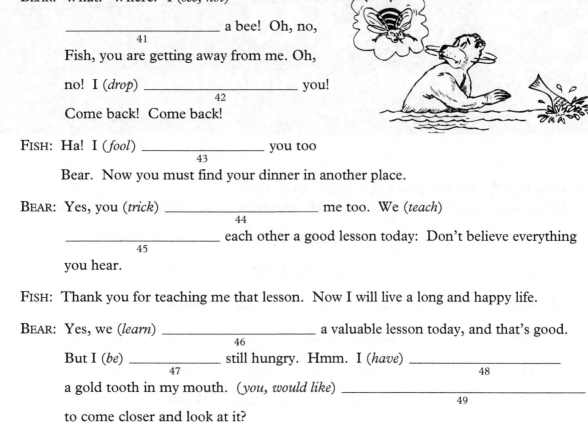

_____ a bee! Oh, no,
         41

Fish, you are getting away from me. Oh,

no! I (*drop*) _____ you!
                 42

Come back! Come back!

FISH: Ha! I (*fool*) _____ you too
             43

Bear. Now you must find your dinner in another place.

BEAR: Yes, you (*trick*) _____ me too. We (*teach*)
             44

_____ each other a good lesson today: Don't believe everything
         45

you hear.

FISH: Thank you for teaching me that lesson. Now I will live a long and happy life.

BEAR: Yes, we (*learn*) _____ a valuable lesson today, and that's good.
             46

But I (*be*) _____ still hungry. Hmm. I (*have*) _____
        47   48

a gold tooth in my mouth. (*you, would like*) _____
                                        49

to come closer and look at it?

Chapter 10

Expressing Future Time, Part 1

▶ **Practice 1. Forms of *be going to*.** (Chart 10-1)
Create your own chart by completing each sentence with the correct form of *be going to*.

Tomorrow

1. I   _____*am going to be*_____ absent.

2. We _____ absent.

3. She _____ absent.

4. You _____ absent.

5. They _____ absent.

6. Tim and I _____ absent.

7. Mr. Han _____ absent.

8. Mr. Han and you _____ absent.

9. He _____ absent.

10. Rick and Sam _____ absent.

▶ **Practice 2. *Be going to*.** (Chart 10-1)
Complete each sentence with the correct form of *be going to*.

1. A: (*you, be*) _____*Are you going to be*_____ at home tomorrow morning around ten?

    B: No. I (*be*) _____ out.

2. A: (*Albert, fix*) _____ the bathroom faucet soon? It's still dripping.

    B: He already tried. I (*call*) _____ a plumber in the morning.

3. A: (*you, apply*) _____ for the security job at the mall?

    B: Yes. I (*complete*) _____ the online application tomorrow.

4. A: (*Ed and Nancy, join*) _____ us at the restaurant for dinner?

    B: Yes, they (*meet*) _____ us there at 7:00.

▶ **Practice 3. *Be going to.*** (Chart 10-1)
Read the story. Rewrite the second paragraph using ***be going to***.

Mondays are always very busy for Antonia. She is the project manager for a construction company, and she has a long day. Here is her schedule.

   She wakes up at 5:00. She has a quick breakfast of toast and coffee. She catches the 5:45 train to work. At 6:30, she has a weekly meeting with her employees. For the rest of the morning, she is at her desk. She answers phone calls and emails, and she works on project details. She answers a lot of questions. She has a big lunch at 11:00. In the afternoon, she visits job sites. She meets with builders and architects. She finishes by 7:00 and is home by 8:00.

   Today is Monday. What is Antonia going to do?

   She is going to wake up at 5:00. She _____

   _____

   _____

   _____

   _____

   _____

   _____

   _____

▶ **Practice 4. *Be going to.*** (Chart 10-1)
Complete the sentences. Use ***be going to*** and the given expressions.

call the neighbors	eat a big lunch	take it back to the store
check the lost-and-found	✓ go back to bed	take some medicine
do a search on the Internet	look for a bigger place	

1. It's 8:00 A.M. and I'm very tired.

   I _____*am going to go back to bed.*_____

2. I'm hungry. I didn't have breakfast.

   I _____

3. I have a stomachache.

   I _____

4. The dog next door is barking loudly.

   I _____

5. Richard needs to get some information about earthquakes for a school project.

   He _____

6. The Smiths have a new baby. Their apartment is too small.

   They _____

7. Diane left her purse in the classroom.

   She _____

8. The zipper broke on my new dress.

   I _____

zipper

▶ **Practice 5. Be going to.** (Chart 10-1)
Write answers to the question **What are you going to do?** Use **be going to** in your answers.

   1. You're thirsty. _____*I am going to get a drink of water.*_____

   2. You have a sore throat. _____

   3. You broke a tooth. _____

   4. Your alarm didn't go off. You are in bed, and class starts in fifteen minutes. _____

   _____

   5. It's midnight. You are wide awake, and you want to go to sleep. _____

   _____

   6. You are at school. You locked your bike in a bike rack, and now it's not there. _____

   _____

▶ **Practice 6. *Be going to:* negative and question forms.** (Chart 10-1)
Create your own chart by rewriting the given sentences as negatives and questions.

	Negative	Question
1. I am going to eat.	*I am not going to eat.*	*Am I going to eat?*
2. You are going to eat.	_____	_____
3. He is going to eat.	_____	_____
4. She is going to eat.	_____	_____
5. We are going to eat.	_____	_____
6. They are going to eat.	_____	_____
7. My friend is going to eat.	_____	_____
8. The students are going to eat.	_____	_____

▶ **Practice 7. *Be going to:* negative and question forms.** (Chart 10-1)
Complete each sentence with the correct form of the verb in parentheses. Use *be going to*.

1. A: What (*you, do*) _____ *are you going to do* _____ next weekend?

   B: We (*go*) _____ fishing at a lake in the mountains.

   A: (*you, stay*) _____ overnight?

   B: No. We (*come*) _____ back the same day.

2. A: Where (*Sally, work*) _____ this summer?

   B: She (*work, not*) _____. She (*take*)
   _____ summer school classes.

3. A: (*the students, have*) _____ an end-of-the-year party?

   B: Yes, they are. They (*have*) _____ a picnic
   at the park near the beach.

4. A: (*Joan and Bob, move*) _____ next month?

   B: Yes. Joan (*start*) _____ a new job in
   the city.

   A: (*they, look for*) _____ a house?

   B: No, they (*look for, not*) _____ a house.
   They (*rent*) _____ an apartment.

▶ **Practice 8. Using the present progressive for future time.** (Chart 10-2)
Rewrite the sentences using the present progressive for the future verbs.

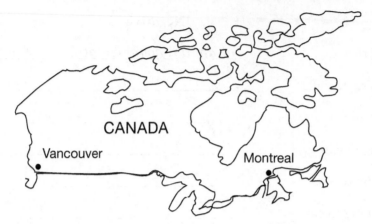

1. The Johnsons are going to take a camping trip across Canada this summer.

    The Johnsons are taking a camping trip across Canada this summer.

2. They are going to take their teenage grandchildren with them.

    _____

3. They are going to stay in parks and campgrounds.

    _____

4. They are going to leave from Vancouver in June.

    _____

5. They are going to arrive in Montreal in August.

    _____

6. Mr. and Mrs. Johnson are going to drive back home alone.

    _____

7. Their grandchildren are going to fly home because they don't want to miss the beginning
   of school.

    _____

    _____

8. Their parents are going to meet them at the airport.

    _____

► **Practice 9. Using the present progressive for future time.** (Chart 10-2)
Write "P" if the sentence has a present meaning. Write "F" if the sentence has a future meaning.

1. ___P___ Wait! I'm coming.

2. _____ I'm coming at 8:00 tonight.

3. _____ Wait—what are you doing?

4. _____ Ron is taking us to the airport soon.

5. _____ I'm returning this library book. I'm sorry it's late.

6. _____ We're flying to Rome in a few weeks.

7. _____ A: Joe, are you leaving?

   _____ B: No, I'm not going. I'm staying.

8. _____ Claude and Marie are spending their next
   vacation hiking in the mountains.

► **Practice 10. Using *yesterday, last, tomorrow, next, in*, or *ago*.** (Chart 10-3)
Complete the phrases with the appropriate time word.

1. I left for my trip . . .

   a. ____*yesterday*____ afternoon.

   b. _____ fall.

   c. _____ week.

   d. _____ weekend.

   e. _____ morning.

   f. two hours _____ .

   g. _____ month.

   h. three months _____ .

   i. _____ night.

   j. _____ evening.

2. Sam is going to leave for his trip . . .

   a. ____*tomorrow*____ afternoon.

   b. _____ fall.

   c. _____ week.

   d. _____ weekend.

   e. _____ morning.

   f. _____ two hours.

   g. _____ month.

   h. _____ three months.

   i. _____ night.

   j. _____ evening.

▶ **Practice 11. Using *yesterday, last, tomorrow, next, in*, or *ago*.** (Chart 10-3)
Complete the sentences. Use *yesterday*, *last*, *tomorrow*, *next*, *in*, or *ago*.

1. I went to Hawaii _____*last*_____ year.

2. I went to Hawaii a year _____.

3. My sister went to Singapore a week _____.

4. My sister went to Singapore _____ week.

5. Our neighbors are going to Iceland _____ Friday.

6. We're going to Morocco _____ two weeks.

7. My parents went to Costa Rica _____ afternoon.

8. Their friends are going to Costa Rica _____ morning.

9. My cousins are going to Kenya _____ three weeks.

10. Were you home _____ afternoon around 4:00?

11. Were you home _____ night around 9:00?

12. Are you going to be in the office _____ afternoon around 3:00?

13. I wasn't at work two days _____.

14. I'm not going to be at work _____ Thursday.

▶ **Practice 12. Using *a couple of* with past and future.** (Chart 10-4)
Check (✓) the expressions that can mean *a couple of*. Rewrite the expressions using *a couple of*.

1. ___✓___ two hours _____*a couple of hours*_____

2. _____ seven minutes _____

3. _____ five days _____

4. _____ six years _____

5. _____ three months _____

6. _____ two years _____

7. _____ four hours _____

8. _____ one minute _____

9. _____ two weeks _____

▶ **Practice 13. Using *a few* with past and future.** (Chart 10-4)
Check (✓) the expressions that can mean *a few*. Rewrite the expressions using *a few*.

1. ___✓___ five minutes   _____a few minutes_____

2. _____ seven months   _____

3. _____ four hours   _____

4. _____ three days   _____

5. _____ ten weeks   _____

6. _____ five years   _____

7. _____ one day   _____

▶ **Practice 14. Using *a couple of* or *a few* with past and future.** (Chart 10-4)
Make sentences using the given words.

1. I \ leave

   a. (*in a few days*)

   _____I am going to leave in a few days._____

   b. (*a few days ago*)

   _____I left a few days ago._____

2. Susie \ marry Paul

   a. (*a couple of months ago*)

   _____

   b. (*in a couple of months*)

   _____

3. Dr. Nelson \ retire

   a. (*a few years ago*)

   _____

   b. (*in a few years*)

   _____

4. Jack \ begin a new job

   a. (*a couple of days ago*)

   _____

   b. (*in a couple of days*)

   _____

▶ **Practice 15. Using *this* with time words and *today* or *tonight*.** (Chart 10-5)
Circle the meaning of each sentence: past, present, or future time.

1.	Tom is going to finish school this June.	past	present	(future)
2.	We took my parents to the airport this morning.	past	present	future
3.	Nancy is at her grandmother's. She is cleaning her house this morning.	past	present	future
4.	Mrs. Andrew had lunch with friends today.	past	present	future
5.	Our secretary is going to retire this month.	past	present	future
6.	The children are studying dinosaurs this month.	past	present	future
7.	I am doing a lot of work today.	past	present	future
8.	We heard about an interesting movie this morning.	past	present	future
9.	You are going to have a good time tonight.	past	present	future
10.	I had fun this evening.	past	present	future
11.	Are you going to be home this afternoon?	past	present	future

▶ **Practice 16. Using time words.** (Chart 10-5)
Read the description of Sophia's morning. Then choose all the correct completions.

It's 6:00 A.M. Sophia is late and needs to hurry. She is taking a shower. Then she is going to get dressed, have breakfast, and go to school.

1. Sophia woke up early	(this morning.)	(today.)	right now.
2. She is late	this morning.	today.	right now.
3. She is going to go to school	this morning.	today.	right now.
4. She is going to have breakfast	this morning.	today.	right now.
5. She is in a hurry	this morning.	today.	right now.
6. She got up before 6:00	this morning.	today.	right now.

▶ **Practice 17. Using *this* with time words.** (Chart 10-5)
Read the story about Sara. Then answer the questions.

    Right now, I'm sitting in my kitchen. I'm thinking about going to school. This morning I woke up late. I overslept and missed my math class. I have an important chemistry test this afternoon. I have a problem. I don't want to miss it, but my chemistry teacher is also my math teacher. I'm not sure what to do. How do I explain my absence from my math class? I'm going to sit at the kitchen table and think about a solution.

1. What are two things Sara did this morning?

    a. _____*She woke up late.*_____

    b. _____

2. What are two things Sara is going to do this morning?

    a. _____

    b. _____

3. What is one thing Sara is doing this morning?

    _____

▶ **Practice 18. Forms of *will*.** (Chart 10-6)
Create your own chart by completing the sentences with the correct forms of *will*.

1. We aren't late.	We	_____*will be*_____	there soon.
2. You aren't late.	You	_____	there soon.
3. They aren't late.	They	_____	there soon.
4. She isn't late.	She	_____	there soon.
5. I'm not late.	I	_____	there soon.
6. The students aren't late.	The students	_____	there soon.
7. My mother isn't late.	My mother	_____	there soon.
8. He isn't late.	He	_____	there soon.
9. Jill and I aren't late.	Jill and I	_____	there soon.
10. Eva and her son aren't late.	Eva and her son	_____	there soon.

► **Practice 19. Using *will*.** (Chart 10-6)
Imagine you are a tourist in San Francisco. What are you going to do? Complete the sentences with ***will*** or ***won't***.

1. I _____ take a tour of the city.

2. I _____ ride a cable car.

3. I _____ walk across the Golden Gate Bridge.

a cable car

4. I _____ practice my English.

5. I _____ speak my own language.

6. I _____ visit the Walt Disney Family Museum.

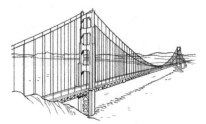

7. I _____ see the famous flower gardens at Golden Gate Park.

8. I _____ walk to the top of Telegraph Hill for beautiful views of the city.

the Golden Gate Bridge

9. I _____ eat fresh seafood at Fisherman's Wharf.

10. I _____ take the ferry to Alcatraz Island.

a ferry to Alcatraz Island

► **Practice 20. Using *will*.** (Chart 10-6)
What will happen fifty years from now? Complete each sentence with ***will*** or ***won't*** and the verb in parentheses.

Fifty years from now . . .

1. most people (*live*) _____ to be 100.

2. people (*travel*) _____ to other planets.

3. students (*study*) _____ at home with computers, not at school.

4. students (*study*) _____ in the classroom.

5. some people (*live*) _____ in underwater homes.

6. scientists (*discover*) _____ cures for serious diseases like cancer and AIDS.

7. there (*be*) _____ wars.

8. the world (*be*) _____ peaceful.

▶ **Practice 21. Will.** (Chart 10-6)
Change the sentences by using **will** to express future time.

1. Class is going to finish a few minutes early today.

    _____*Class will finish a few minutes early today.*_____

2. You are going to need extra chairs for the party.

    _____

3. Hurry or we aren't going to be on time for the movie.

    _____

4. Your brother and sister are going to help you with your science project.

    _____

5. The bus isn't going to be on time today.

    _____

6. Watch out! You're going to cut yourself with that sharp knife.

    _____

7. Carlos and Olivia are going to graduate from nursing school with high grades.

    _____

▶ **Practice 22. Questions with will.** (Chart 10-7)
Make questions using the given words.

In the future

1. you \ live to be 100 years old?

    _____*Will you live to be 100 years old?*_____

2. your friends \ live to be 100 years old?

    _____

3. your children \ live to be 100 years old?

_____

4. we \ live on another planet?

_____

5. my friends \ live on another planet?

_____

6. some people \ live underwater?

_____

7. I \ live underwater?

_____

8. countries \ find a solution for poverty?

_____

▶ **Practice 23. Forms of _be going to_ and _will_.** (Chart 10-8)
Complete each sentence with the correct form of the verb.

| _be going to_ + _go_ | _will_ + _go_ |

Statement

1. I ____am going to go____ .   I ____will go____ .

2. You _____ .   You _____ .

3. The students _____ .   The students _____ .

4. Ms. Jenkins _____ .   Ms. Jenkins _____ .

5. Our friends _____ .   Our friends _____ .

Negative

6. Mr. Davis (_not_) _____ .   Mr. Davis (_not_) _____ .

7. I (_not_) _____ .   I (_not_) _____ .

8. We (_not_) _____ .   We (_not_) _____ .

Question

9. (_she, go_) _____ ?   (_she, go_) _____ ?

10. (_they, go_) _____ ?   (_they, go_) _____ ?

11. (_you, go_) _____ ?   (_you, go_) _____ ?

► **Practice 24. Verb review: present, past, and future.** (Chart 10-8)
Make questions with the given words. Use **will** for future tense.

1. you \ need \ help \ now?

    Do you need help now?

2. you \ need \ help \ tomorrow?

    _____

3. you \ need \ help \ yesterday?

    _____

4. Eva \ need \ help \ yesterday?

    _____

5. Eva \ need \ help \ tomorrow?

    _____

6. Eva \ need \ help \ now?

    _____

7. the students \ need \ help \ now?

    _____

8. the students \ need \ help \ tomorrow?

    _____

9. the students \ need \ help \ yesterday?

    _____

► **Practice 25. Verb review: present, past, and future.** (Chart 10-8)
Complete each sentence with the correct form of the verb in parentheses.

1. Right now, Noor (*eat*) _____ _is eating_ _____ fish for lunch.

2. She (*eat*) _____ fish for lunch once or twice a week.

3. She also (*eat*) _____ chicken often.

4. She usually (*have*) _____ chicken for dinner.

5. Last night Noor (*cook*) _____ a spicy chicken and rice dish for her
   friends.

6. It (*be*) _____ delicious, and they (*love*) _____ it.

7. While she was cooking dinner, she (*drop*)

   _____ a pan of hot oil on the floor, but

   fortunately she (*be*) _____ okay.

   It (*burn, not*) _____ her.

8. Tomorrow Noor (*invite*) _____ her

   parents over for lunch.

9. (*she, cook*) _____ fish?

10. (*she, make*) _____ chicken?

11. Maybe she (*prepare, not*) _____ chicken

    or fish.

12. Maybe she (*surprise*) _____ her parents

    with a completely new dish.

▶ **Practice 26. Verb review: *be*** (Chart 10-9)
Make sentences with the given words.

1. you \ be \ sick \ now?

   _____ *Are you sick now?* _____

2. you \ be \ sick \ tomorrow?

   _____

3. you \ be \ sick \ yesterday?

   _____

4. Steve \ be \ sick \ yesterday?

   _____

5. Steve \ be \ sick \ tomorrow?

   _____

6. Steve \ be \ sick \ now?

   _____

7. your kids \ be \ sick \ now?

   _____

8. your kids \ be \ sick \ tomorrow?

_____

9. your kids \ be \ sick \ yesterday?

_____

▶ **Practice 27. Verb review: be.** (Chart 10-9)
Complete each sentence with the correct form of the verb in parentheses.

1. I (*be*) _____*am*_____ very busy today. Right now, I (*be*) _____ in
   Quebec. Tomorrow I (*be*) _____ in New York. Yesterday I (*be*)
   _____ in Paris. I (*be*) _____ home next week.

2. A: Where (*you, be*) _____ last night? (*you, be*) _____
      _____ at home?

   B: No, I (*be, not*) _____. I (*be*) _____ at the library with my
      friends.

   A: I (*be*) _____ there too. Where (*you, be*) _____?

   B: We (*be*) _____ in the study area.

   A: Oh. I (*be*) _____ in the reference section.

3. A: (*the post office, be*) _____ open now?

   B: No, it (*be, not*) _____. Today (*be*) _____ a national
      holiday.

   A: What about banks? (*they, be*) _____ open?

   B: No, they (*be, not*) _____. All the banks (*be*) _____ closed.

▶ **Practice 28. Simple present questions.** (Charts 10-8 and 10-9)
Complete the sentences with **are** or **do**.

Isabella is starting a new job this morning. Her mother is asking her questions on the phone.

1. _____*Do*_____ you need to get there early?

2. _____ you nervous or excited?

3. _____ you feel nervous or excited?

4. _____ you know your co-workers' names?

5. _____ you ready to begin?

6. _____ you need ID?

7. _____ you have your cell phone?

8. _____ you taking the bus or subway?

9. _____ you want me to call you later?

▶ **Practice 29. Simple past questions.** (Charts 10-8 and 10-9)
Complete the sentences with *were* or *did*.
Dan had an important math test this morning. A friend is asking him about it.

1. _____*Did*_____ you study for the test last night?

2. _____ you get enough sleep?

3. _____ you nervous this morning?

4. _____ you ready for the test?

5. _____ you do well?

6. _____ you make any mistakes?

7. _____ you get 100%?

8. _____ you happy when you finished?

▶ **Practice 30. Verb review: present, past, and future.** (Charts 10-8 and 10-9)
Complete the chart with the correct forms of the verbs.

Every Day / Now	Yesterday	Tomorrow
1. I **drink** tea every day. I _____*am drinking*_____ tea now.	I _____*drank*_____ tea yesterday.	I _____*am going to drink*_____ tea tomorrow. I _____*will drink*_____ tea tomorrow.
2. We **work** every day. We _____ now.	We _____ yesterday.	We _____ tomorrow. We _____ tomorrow.
3. She **is** late every day. She _____ late now.	She _____ late yesterday.	She _____ late tomorrow. She _____ late tomorrow.
4. You _____ me every day. You _____ me now.	You **helped** me yesterday.	You _____ me tomorrow. You _____ me tomorrow.

Every Day / Now	Yesterday	Tomorrow
5. She **doesn't come** every day. She _____ now.	She _____ yesterday.	She _____ tomorrow. She _____ tomorrow.
6. She _____ the dishes every day. She **isn't doing** the dishes now.	She _____ the dishes yesterday.	She _____ the dishes tomorrow. She _____ the dishes tomorrow.
7. _____ every day? **Are they exercising** now?	_____ yesterday?	_____ tomorrow? _____ tomorrow?
8. _____ on time every day? _____ on time now?	**Was he** on time yesterday?	_____ on time tomorrow? _____ on time tomorrow?
9. She **isn't** on time every day. She _____ on time now.	She _____ on time yesterday.	She _____ on time tomorrow. She _____ on time tomorrow.

▶ **Practice 31. Verb review: past, present, and future.** (Charts 10-8 and 10-9)
Complete the sentences. Use the words in parentheses. Use any appropriate verb form.

1. A: I (lose) _____*lost*_____ my sunglasses yesterday.

   B: Where?

   A: I probably (leave) _____ them on a table at the restaurant.

2. A: What (you, wear) _____ to the party next weekend?

   B: I (wear) _____ my jeans. It (be) _____
   _____ a casual party.

3. A: Sometimes children tell little lies. You talked to Annie. (she, tell)
   _____ the truth, or (she, tell) _____ a lie?

   B: She (tell) _____ the truth. She's honest.

4. A: How are you getting along?

   B: Fine. (I, make) _____ a lot of friends, and my English (get)
   _____ better.

5. A: What are you going to do tonight? (*you, study*) _____
   _____?

   B: No. I (*have, not*) _____ any homework.

   A: Really?

   B: Our teacher (*give*) _____ us a lot of work last week. She (*give*)
   _____ us a break this week.

6. A: Mark's wedding is next weekend. (*you, be*) _____
   there?

   B: No. I have to take my dad home from the hospital on Saturday. He (*have*)
   _____ surgery in a few days.

   A: Really? That's too bad.

   B: He (*break*) _____ his leg last year, and it (*heal, not*)
   _____ properly.

7. A: Good morning.

   B: Excuse me?

   A: I (*say*) _____, "Good morning."

   B: Oh! Good morning! I'm sorry. I (*understand, not*)
   _____ at first.

8. A: Where (*Cathy, be*) _____? I need to talk to her.

   B: She (*meet*) _____ with some students right now.

9. I almost (*have*) _____ an accident yesterday. A dog (*run*)
   _____ into the street in front of my car. I (*slam*) _____
   on my brakes and just (*miss*) _____ the dog.

10. A: (*you, call*) _____ George tomorrow? It's his birthday.

    B: Thank you for the reminder! I always (*forget*) _____ his birthday.

▶ **Practice 32. Verb review: past, present, and future.** (Charts 10-8 and 10-9)
Choose the correct verbs.

Jack and the Beanstalk

A long time ago, a boy named Jack (*is living / lived*) with his mother. They (*are / were*) very
                                                          1   2
poor. They (*didn't have / don't have*) money for food. His mother (*decided / was deciding*) to sell
               3   4
their cow.

So, Jack (*is taking / took*) the cow to town. He (*met / was meeting*) a man. The man said,
              5   6
"I (*buy / will buy*)" your cow. I (*will give / give*) you magic beans. Jack (*took / was taking*) the
        7   8   9
beans to his mother. She (*was / did*) very angry. She said, "You (*be / are*) a stupid boy. Now
                                10   11
we (*don't have / not have*) anything."
        12

Before he went to bed, Jack (*threw / is throwing*) the beans out the window. The next
                                      13
morning, he (*was seeing / saw*) a big beanstalk outside his window. He (*climbed / is climbing*) it
                    14   15
and (*found / was finding*) a castle. A giant's wife told him, "You need to hide. My husband
          16
(*eats / will eat*) you for breakfast." She hid Jack in the oven.
    17

The giant smelled Jack. He asked his wife, "(*Are you going to give / Do you give*) me a boy
                                                                      18
for breakfast? She answered, "No, that smell (*is / will be*) the boy from last week."
                                                      19

After the giant (*fell / is going to fall*) asleep, Jack took some of the giant's money
                        20
and escaped.

His mother (*did / was*) very happy. She (*didn't want / no want*)
                  21   22
Jack to go back to the castle. But Jack (*was going / went*)
                                              23
back to the castle two more times. He got a hen, golden eggs,
and a harp.

The giant (*never caught / is never catching*) Jack. The giant
                    24
(*is going to run / ran*) after Jack, but Jack chopped down the
        25
beanstalk and the giant (*died / was dying*).
                              26

Jack and his mother (*lives / lived*) happily ever after.
                          27

a castle

a beanstalk

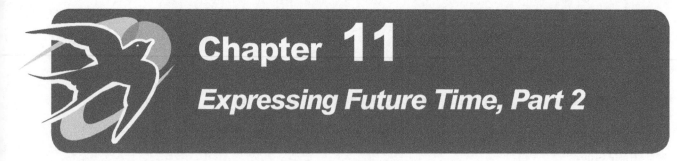

Chapter 11

Expressing Future Time, Part 2

▶ **Practice 1. *May*, *might*, or *will*.** (Chart 11-1)
Circle the meaning of each sentence: sure or unsure.

1.	It may be stormy tomorrow.	sure	(unsure)
2.	I will be absent next week.	sure	unsure
3.	Joe and Jeff won't be at work tomorrow.	sure	unsure
4.	We might take a trip next week.	sure	unsure
5.	Sandra may take a vacation soon.	sure	unsure
6.	We won't go camping next week.	sure	unsure
7.	Our English class may get together for dinner soon.	sure	unsure
8.	Some of our teachers might be there.	sure	unsure
9.	Some of our teachers won't be there.	sure	unsure

▶ **Practice 2. *May*, *might*, or *will*.** (Chart 11-1)
Complete the sentences with *may*, *might*, *will*, or *won't* and the verb in parentheses. Give your own opinion.

One hundred years from now, . . .

1. the earth (*be*) _____ very hot.

2. cars (*fly*) _____ .

3. people (*travel*) _____ easily to space.

4. all school courses (*be*) _____ online.

5. there (*be*) _____ enough food and water for everyone in the world.

6. 100% of our energy for electricity (*come*) _____ from the sun.

7. everyone (*speak*) _____ the same language.

8. everyone (*live*) _____ in peace.

▶ **Practice 3. Maybe vs. may be.** (Chart 11-2)
Make sentences using the given words.

1. It \ be \ sunny tomorrow

    a. (*may*) _____It may be sunny tomorrow._____

    b. (*maybe*) _Maybe it will be sunny tomorrow._____

2. You \ need to see \ a doctor soon

    a. (*might*) _____

    b. (*maybe*) _____

3. We \ play \ basketball after school

    a. (*may*) _____

    b. (*might*) _____

4. Our class \ go \ to a movie together

    a. (*maybe*) _____

    b. (*may*) _____

▶ **Practice 4. Maybe vs. may be.** (Chart 11-2)
Circle the letters of the correct sentences. In some cases, both sentences may be correct.

1. ⓐ I may need your advice.
   ⓑ Maybe I will need your advice.

2. a. The teacher may give a surprise quiz tomorrow.
   b. The teacher maybe will give a surprise quiz tomorrow.

3. a. Maybe all the students do well.
   b. Maybe all the students will do well.

4. a. Maybe traffic will be heavy later.
   b. Maybe traffic is heavy later.

5. a. You may will need more time.
   b. Maybe you will need more time.

6. a. We may delay our trip for a few days.
   b. Maybe we will delay our trip for a few days.

7. a. Maybe they are come.
   b. Maybe they will come.

▶ **Practice 5. *May, might,* and *maybe.*** (Charts 11-1 and 11-2)
Rewrite the given sentences.

Tomorrow	May	Might
1. Maybe I will come.	*I may come.*	*I might come.*
2. Maybe they will come.	_____	_____

	Might	May
3. Maybe she won't study.	_____	_____
4. Maybe we won't need help.	_____	_____
5. Maybe I won't need help.	_____	_____

	May	Maybe
6. He might understand.	_____	_____
7. You might understand.	_____	_____
8. They might understand.	_____	_____

▶ **Practice 6. Review: *Maybe, may, might,* and *will.*** (Chart 11-2)
Make sentences with the given words and the ideas in parentheses. Use ***maybe***, ***may***, ***might***, or ***will***.

1. It \ snow \ tomorrow (*you are sure*)

    It will snow tomorrow.

2. It \ snow \ next week (*you are unsure*)

    _____

3. We \ go ice-skating on the lake (*you are unsure*)

    _____

4. The kids \ play in the snow (*you are sure*)

    _____

5. The snow \ melt, not \ for several days (*you are sure*)

    _____

► **Practice 7. Review: *Maybe, may, might,* and *will*.** (Chart 11-2)
Choose all the grammatically correct sentences.

1. (a.) Maybe I am going to skip class tomorrow.
   b. Maybe I skip class tomorrow.
   (c.) I might skip class tomorrow.
   (d.) Maybe I will skip class tomorrow.

2. a. It will snow in the mountains next week.
   b. It might snow in the mountains next week.
   c. Maybe it snows in the mountains next week.
   d. Maybe it will snow in the mountains next week.

3. a. We may not have a warm summer this year.
   b. We won't have a warm summer this year.
   c. Maybe we won't have a warm summer this year.
   d. Maybe we don't have a warm summer this year.

4. a. Maybe you are need extra time for the test tomorrow.
   b. You might need extra time for the test tomorrow.
   c. You may be need extra time for the test tomorrow.
   d. Maybe you will need extra time for the test tomorrow.

► **Practice 8. *Before* and *after*.** (Chart 11-3)
Look at the pairs of sentences. Decide which action happens first and which happens second.
Then write two sentences: one with ***before*** and one with ***after***. Use a form of ***be going to*** in
the main clause.

1. ___*1*___ I boil the water.

   ___*2*___ I put in the rice.

   a. _____*Before I put in the rice, I am going to boil the water.*_____

   b. _____*After I boil the water, I am going to put in the rice.*_____

2. _____ I turn in my homework.

   _____ I check my answers.

   a. _____

   b. _____

3. _____ I wash the dishes.

_____ I clear off the table.

a. _____

b. _____

4. _____ I get my umbrella.

_____ I go out in the rain.

a. _____

b. _____

5. _____ I board the airplane.

_____ I go to the departure gate.

a. _____

b. _____

▶ **Practice 9. *Before, after,* and *when.*** (Chart 11-3)
Write logical sentences with the given words.

Carlos is a student. What is he going to do tomorrow?

1. make breakfast \ get up

   After ____*he gets up, he is going to make breakfast.*_____

2. eat breakfast \ go to school

   Before _____

3. go to his classroom \ get to school

   After _____

4. have lunch in the cafeteria \ talk to his friends

   When _____

5. cook dinner for his roommates \ pick up food at the grocery store

   Before _____

6. do his homework \ go to bed

   Before _____

7. fall asleep \ have good dreams

   After _____

▶ **Practice 10. *Before, after,* and *when*.** (Chart 11-3)
Complete each sentence with the verb in parentheses. Use ***be going to*** for future.

1. Before I (*fix*)_____*fix*_____ dinner tonight, I (*get*) _____*am going to get*_____
   fresh vegetables from my garden.

2. After I (*have*) _____ dinner, I (*go*) _____ out with
   friends for dessert.

3. When I (*see*) _____ my friends, we (*make*) _____
   plans for a camping trip this summer.

4. Before Susan (*take*) _____ the driving test next week, she (*practice*)
   _____ with her parents.

5. When Susan (*take*) _____ the test next week, she (*feel*)
   _____ nervous.

6. After Susan (*get*) _____ her license, she (*be*) _____ a
   careful driver.

▶ **Practice 11. Clauses with *if*.** (Chart 11-4)
Complete each sentence with the correct verb in parentheses.

1. If Ellen (*wins, will win*) _____*wins*_____ a scholarship, she
   (*attends, will attend*) _____*will attend*_____ a four-year college or university.

2. If she (*goes, will go*) _____ to a college or university, she
   (*is going to study, studies*) _____ chemistry.

3. If she (*enjoys, will enjoy*) _____ chemistry, she (*takes, will take*)
   _____ pre-med* courses.

4. She (*applies, will apply*) _____ to medical school if she
   (*is going to do, does*) _____ well in her pre-med courses.

_____

pre-med = classes that prepare a student for medical school.

5. If she (*attends, will attend*) _____ medical school, she

(*studies, is going to study*) _____ family medicine.

6. If she (*completes, is going to complete*) _____ her training, she

(*works, is going to work*) _____ around the world helping people.

▶ **Practice 12. Clauses with *if*.** (Chart 11-4)
Complete each sentence with the verb in parentheses.

1. If it (*be*) _____*is*_____ sunny tomorrow, Jake (*spend*) ___*is going to spend*___ OR

_____*will spend*_____ the day at the beach.

2. If it (*rain*) _____ tomorrow, I (*spend, not*)

_____ the day at the beach.

3. If Beth (*get*) _____ a high score on her college entrance exams, her

parents (*be*) _____ proud of her.

4. Her parents (*get*) _____ her extra help if she (*do, not*) _____

well.

5. If Mark (*get*) _____ a job as a tour guide this summer, he (*earn*)

_____ enough money for school next year.

6. If Mark (*get, not*) _____ a good job, he (*delay*) _____

_____ school for a year.

7. If Lesley (*feel*) _____ sick tomorrow, she (*come, not*) _____

_____ to school.

8. She (*call*) _____ you for the homework assignments if she (*miss*)

_____ class.

9. If Brian (*need*) _____ help this weekend, we (*help*) _____ him.

10. We (*make*) _____ other plans if he (*need, not*) _____

help next week.

▶ **Practice 13. *Before, after,* and *if*.** (Charts 11-3 and 11-4)
Complete the sentences with the words in parentheses.

On Ana's birthday, Alex is going to ask Ana to marry him.

He (*ask*) _*is going to ask / will ask*_ her after they
                                    1

(*celebrate*) _____*celebrate*_____ her birthday at a
                          2

restaurant. Before Alex (*talk*) _____ to Ana,
                                              3

he (*meet*) _____ with her parents.
                        4

If they (*agree*) _____, Alex (*buy*) _____
                               5   6
an engagement ring for Ana. If Ana (*say*) _____ "yes,"
                                                                  7
Alex (*surprise*) _____ her with the ring. If Ana (*say, not*)
                            8
_____ "yes," Alex (*save*) _____ the ring and try
            9   10
again later.

▶ **Practice 14. Time clauses and questions.** (Charts 11-3 and 11-4)
Read the story about Frank. Write questions with ***will***. Then give short answers using ***will*** or
won't.

   Frank has a good job as an IT* employee. He is the owner's son, but he is lazy. His co-
workers don't like to work with him. His father is going to fire him if he doesn't change his
work habits. Beginning Monday, Frank is going to get to work on time. He isn't going to stay
up late the night before work. He isn't going to fall asleep at his desk. He is going to read all
his emails before he deletes them. He is going to answer his phone and check his voice mails.
He is going to help his co-workers when they ask. He isn't going to tell them he is too busy.
His father and co-workers are going to be happy with Frank's work.

1. change his behavior

    Will he change his behavior? Yes, he will. _____

2. get to work on time

    _____

    _____

───────────────────────────────

*IT = information technology.

3. stay awake at work

_____

4. delete emails before he reads them

_____

5. answer his phone

_____

6. help his co-workers when they ask

_____

7. tell his co-workers he is too busy

_____

8. his father and co-workers be happy

_____

▶ **Practice 15. Habitual present.** (Chart 11-5)
Make sentences using the habitual present.

Part I. Match each word or phrase in Column A with a phrase in Column B. Write the letter in the blank.

Column A

1. __*f*__ drink too much coffee

2. _____ cry

3. _____ not pay my electric bill

4. _____ the phone rings in the middle of the night

5. _____ get to work late

6. _____ have a big breakfast

7. _____ not do my homework

Column B

a. my eyes get red

b. stay at work late

c. not answer it

d. get low grades on the tests

e. have no electricity

✓ f. feel shaky and nervous

g. have a lot of energy

Part II. Now, write habitual present sentences beginning with *If I* . . . .

1. ___*If I drink too much coffee, I feel shaky and nervous.*___

2. _____

3. _____

4. _____

5. _____

6. _____

7. _____

▶ **Practice 16. Habitual present.** (Chart 11-5)
Answer the questions. Pay special attention to punctuation.

1. How do you feel if you're late for class?

   a. _____*If I'm late for class, I feel nervous.*_____

   b. _____*I feel nervous if I'm late for class.*_____

2. How do you feel after you eat too much?

   a. After _____

   _____

   b. _____

   after _____

3. What do you do if you get a headache?

   a. If _____

   b. _____ if _____

4. What do you do when your teacher talks too fast?

   a. When _____

   b. _____ when _____

▶ **Practice 17. Habitual present vs. future.** (Chart 11-5)
Circle *present habit* or *future* for each sentence.

1. When I'm tired, I take a nap.	(present habit) future
2. If I'm tired, I'm going to take a nap.	present habit future
3. After the café closes, the manager will clean the kitchen.	present habit future
4. After the café closes, the manager cleans the kitchen.	present habit future
5. Before I get up, I listen to the news on the radio.	present habit future

6. When Nancy moves to the city, she is going to sell
   her car.   present habit   future

7. Tim is going to check out of his hotel room before
   he has breakfast.   present habit   future

8. When Tim goes to the airport, he takes a taxi.   present habit   future

9. After Tim checks out of his hotel, he will call for
   a taxi.   present habit   future

▶ **Practice 18. Habitual present vs. future.** (Chart 11-5)
   Complete the sentences with the words in parentheses. Use **be going to** for future.

1. My friends and I (*like*) _____*like*_____ to go swimming in the lake if the weather (*be*)
   _____*is*_____ warm.

2. We (*go*) _____ swimming tomorrow if the weather (*be*)
   _____ warm.

3. Before I (*go*) _____ to class today, I (*meet*) _____
   my friends for coffee.

4. Before I (*go*) _____ to my first class, I (*meet, usually*)
   _____ my friends in the cafeteria.

5. I (*buy*) _____ some stamps when I (*go*) _____
   to the post office this afternoon.

6. Jim (*be*) _____ often tired when he (*get*) _____ home from
   work. If he (*feel*) _____ tired, he (*exercise*) _____ for thirty
   minutes. After he (*exercise*) _____, he (*begin*) _____ to feel
   better.

7. If I (*be*) _____ tired tonight, I (*exercise, not*) _____.
   I need to work late at the office tonight.

8. When Mrs. Rose (*travel*) _____ by plane, she
   (*bring*) _____ her own snacks.

9. When she (*travel*) _____ to New York next
   week, she (*pack*) _____ enough food for lunch
   and dinner.

10. Jane is usually on time for appointments. When she (*be*) _____
    late for an appointment, she (*begin*) _____ to feel nervous.

11. Jane is late for work now. She is stuck in traffic. When she (*get*) _____ to
    work, she (*tell*) _____ her co-workers about the heavy traffic.

▶ **Practice 19. What + do.** (Chart 11-6)
Make questions for the given answers using a form of **do**.

1. <u>   *What are they doing*   </u> now? They're taking a break.

2. _____ yesterday? They took a break.

3. _____ tomorrow? They're going to take a break.

4. _____ tomorrow? They will take a break.

5. _____ at 11:00 every day? They take a break.

6. _____ now? He's meeting with the teacher now.

7. _____ last week? We studied at the library.

8. _____ next week? Mara is going to quit her job.

9. _____ next week? I'm going to apply for Mara's job.

10. _____? I work at a hotel. I'm an assistant manager.

11. _____? Carlo is a chef at a five-star restaurant.

▶ **Practice 20. Asking about jobs.** (Chart 11-6)
Make questions for the given answers using a form of *do*.

an electrician   an auto mechanic   a dental assistant

1. _____*What does he do?*_____ He's an electrician.

2. _____ I'm an auto mechanic.

3. _____ We're college students.

4. _____ They're dental assistants.

5. _____ She's an airline pilot.

6. _____ Thomas and Joanne are
   engineers.

7. _____ You're a truck driver.

▶ **Practice 21. Review.** (Chapters 10 and 11)
Choose the correct completion.

1. A: Is Ryan going to come with us to the soccer game this afternoon?
   B: I'm not sure. He _____ come.
   a. is going to   (b.) may   c. maybe   d. will

2. A: Are you going to be home for your vacation?
   B: No, I _____ be home. I'm going to stay with my cousins in Toronto.
   a. will   b. might   c. won't   d. don't

3. A: When _____ your parents going to be here?
   B: In a few minutes.
   a. will   b. do   c. are   d. is

4. A: Do you like all the traveling you do for your job?
   B: Yes. When I'm in a new city, I always _____ new things to see and do.
   a. discover   b. discovering   c. discovers   d. will discover

5. A: What _____ Andrew do?
   B: He's a salesperson at a computer store.
   a. is   b. did   c. will   d. does

6. A: When are you going to pick up the clothes at the dry cleaners?

   B: In a little while. I'm going to stop there before I _____ the kids at school.

      a. pick up   b. will pick up   c. picked up   d. am going to pick up

7. A: Why is the dog barking?

   B: I don't know. _____ someone is outside.

      a. May   b. Is   c. Maybe   d. Did

8. A: When Chen _____ to Taiwan next month, who will he stay with?

   B: I think his sister, but I'm not completely sure.

      a. will go   b. go   c. goes   d. going

▶ **Practice 22. Review.** (Chapters 8 → 11)
Complete each sentence with any appropriate form of the given verbs. Use *be going to* for future.

1. A: (*you, stay*) _____ here during vacation next week?

   B: No. I (*take*) _____ a trip to Montreal. I (*visit*) _____ my cousins.

   A: How long (*you, be*) _____ away?

   B: About five days.

2. A: Is Carol here?

   B: No, she (*be, not*) _____. She (*leave*) _____ a few minutes ago.

   A: (*she, be*) _____ back soon?

   B: I think so.

   A: Where (*she, go*) _____?

   B: She (*go*) _____ to the drugstore.

3. A: Why (*you, wear*) _____ a cast on your foot?

   B: I (*break*) _____ my ankle.

   A: How?

   B: I (*step*) _____ into a hole while I was running in the park.

   a cast

4. A: (*you, see*) _____ Romero tomorrow?

   B: No, I (*have, not*) _____ time.

A: (*you, see*) _____ him any time this week?

B: Maybe Friday.

A: Could you give him this book? I (*borrow*) _____ it a few months
ago and (*forget*) _____ to return it.

B: Sure.

▶ **Practice 23. Review.** (Chapters 8 → 11)
Complete the sentences with the words in parentheses. Use any appropriate verb form. For
future, use **be going to**.

Part I.

Peter and Rachel are brother and sister. Right now their parents (be) _____
                                                                                        1
abroad on a trip, so they (stay) _____ *with their grandmother. They* (like)
                                                              2
_____ *to stay with her. She* (make, always) _____
              3   4
wonderful food for them. And she (tell) _____ *them stories every night before they* (go)
                                                    5
_____ *to bed.*
        6

Before Peter and Rachel (go) _____ *to bed last night, they* (ask)
                                                    7
_____ *their grandmother to tell them a story. She* (agree) _____. *The*
              8   9
children (put) _____ *on their pajamas,* (brush) _____ *their teeth, and*
                              10   11
(sit) _____ *with their grandmother in her big chair to listen to the story.*
              12

Part II.

GRANDMA: That's good. Sit here beside me and get comfortable.

CHILDREN: What (*you, tell*) _____ us about tonight, Grandma?
                                                    13
GRANDMA: Before I (*begin*) _____ the story, I (*give*) _____ each
                                        14   15
of you a kiss on the forehead because I love you very much.

CHILDREN: We (*love*) _____ you too, Grandma.
                                        16

GRANDMA: Tonight I (*tell*) _____ you a story about Rabbit and Eagle.
17
Ready?

CHILDREN: Yes!

GRANDMA: Rabbit had light gray fur and a white tail. He lived with his family in a hole in a
big, grassy field. Rabbit (*be*) _____ afraid of many things, but he (*be*) _____
18   19
especially afraid of Eagle. Eagle liked to eat rabbits for dinner. One day while Rabbit was
eating grass in the field, he (*see*) _____ Eagle in the sky above him. Rabbit (*be*)
20
_____ very afraid and (*run*) _____ home to his hole as fast as he could.
21   22
Rabbit (*stay*) _____ in his hole day after day because he (*be*)
23
_____ afraid to go outside. He (*get*) _____ very hungry, but still he (*stay*)
24   25
_____ in his hole. Finally, he (*find*) _____ the courage to go
26   27
outside because he (*need*) _____ (*eat*) _____.
28   29
Carefully and slowly, he (*put*) _____ his little pink nose outside the hole. He
30
(*smell, not*) _____ any dangerous animals. And he (*see, not*)
31
_____ Eagle anywhere, so he (*hop*) _____ out and (*find*)
32   33
_____ some delicious new grass to eat. While he was eating the grass, he (*see*)
34
_____ a shadow on the field and (*look*) _____ up. It was Eagle! Rabbit
35   36
said, "Please don't eat me, Eagle! Please don't eat me!"

Part III.

GRANDMA: On this sunny afternoon, Eagle was on her way home to her nest when she
(*hear*) _____ a faint sound below her. "What is that sound?" Eagle said
37
to herself. She looked around, but she (*see, not*) _____ anything. She
38
(*decide*) _____ to ignore the sound and go home. She was tired and (*want*)
39
_____ (*rest*) _____ in her nest.
40   41

Then below her, Rabbit (*say*) _____ again in a very loud voice, "Please don't eat
42
me, Eagle! Please don't eat me!"

This time Eagle (*hear*) _____ Rabbit clearly. Eagle (*spot*) _____
43   44
Rabbit in the field, (*fly*) _____ down, and (*pick*) _____ Rabbit up in her
45   46
talons.

"Thank you, Rabbit," said Eagle. "I was hungry and (*know, not*) _____
47
where I could find my dinner. It's a good thing you called to me." Then Eagle (*eat*)
_____ Rabbit for dinner.
48

Part IV.

GRANDMA: There's a lesson to learn from this story, children. If you (*be*) _____
49
afraid and expect bad things to happen, bad things will happen. The opposite is also true.

If you (*expect*) _____ good things to happen, good things will happen. (*you,*
50
understand) _____?
51

Now it's time for bed.

CHILDREN: Please tell us another story!

GRANDMA: Not tonight. I'm tired. After I (*have*) _____ a warm drink, I (*go*)
52
_____ to bed. All of us need (*get*) _____ a good night's sleep.
53   54
Tomorrow (*be*) _____ a busy day.
55

CHILDREN: What (*we, do*) _____ tomorrow?
56

GRANDMA: After we (*have*) _____ breakfast, we (*go*) _____
57   58
to the zoo at Woodland Park. When we (*be*) _____ at the zoo, we (*see*)
59
_____ lots of wonderful animals. Then in the afternoon we
60

(see) _____ a play at the Children's Theater. But before we (see) _____
       61   62
the play, we (have) _____ a picnic lunch in the park.

CHILDREN: Wow! We (have) _____ a wonderful day tomorrow!
                                           64

GRANDMA: Now off to bed! Goodnight, Rachel and Peter. Sleep tight.*

CHILDREN: Goodnight, Grandma. Thank you for the story!

---

* *Sleep tight* means "Sleep well. Have a good night's sleep."

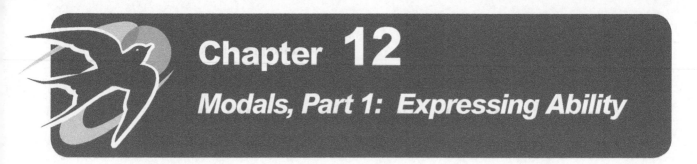

Chapter 12

Modals, Part 1: Expressing Ability

▶ **Practice 1. Can.** (Chart 12-1)
Create your own chart by completing each sentence with the correct form of **can + speak**.

1. I _____ *can speak* _____ some English.

2. You _____ some English.

3. He _____ some English.

4. She _____ some English.

5. We _____ some English.

6. They _____ some English.

7. Tim and I _____ some English.

8. You and your friend _____ some English.

9. My teacher _____ some English.

10. The Yangs _____ some English.

11. Mrs. Vu _____ some English.

▶ **Practice 2. Can or can't.** (Chart 12-1)
Choose the correct answer in each sentence.

1. Dogs (*can*/ *can't*) swim.

2. Dogs (*can* / *can't*) climb trees.

3. Cars (*can* / *can't*) fly.

4. Machines (*can* / *can't*) talk.

5. People (*can* / *can't*) solve problems.

6. Animals (*can* / *can't*) communicate with other animals.

► **Practice 3. *Can* or *can't*.** (Chart 12-1)
Make sentences about what you and other people *can* and *can't* do. Use words from the box or your own words.

do algebra	play the guitar	sail a sailboat	read Chinese characters
fly an airplane	repair a computer	run fast	speak two languages fluently

1. I _____ .

2. I _____ .

3. I _____ .

4. My best friend _____ .

5. My best friend _____ .

6. My (*a person in your family*) _____ .

7. My (*a person in your family*) _____ .

8. My teacher _____ .

► **Practice 4. *Can* or *can't*.** (Charts 12-1 and 12-3)
Make questions and answers using the given information.

	Mia	George	Paul	Eva
drive a car	yes	yes	no	no
play the piano	no	yes	yes	yes
repair a bike	yes	no	yes	no
swim	yes	yes	yes	yes

1. Mia \ repair a bike _____*Can Mia repair a bike? Yes, she can.*_____

2. George and Eva \ play the piano _____

3. George \ drive a car _____

4. Paul \ play the piano _____

5. Mia, George, and Paul \ swim _____

6. Paul and Eva \ drive a car _____

7. Eva and George \ repair a bike _____

8. Eva, Paul, and George \ play the piano _____

▶ **Practice 5. *Can* or *can't*.** (Charts 12-1 and 12-3)
Read the help-wanted ad and look at John's skills. Write interview questions and answers
using the given information. Use *can* or *can't*.

**JOB OPENING AT SMALL
INTERNATIONAL HOTEL**

Looking for person with the following:
good typing and word-processing
skills, excellent knowledge of
English, friendly manner on the
phone. Also needs to help guests
with their suitcases and be available
weekends.

John can: _____✓_____ type

_____✓_____ do word processing

_____ speak English

_____ lift suitcases

_____✓_____ work weekends

	Hotel Manager's Questions	**John's Answers**
1.	*Can you type?*	*Yes, I can.*
2.	_____	_____
3.	_____	_____
4.	_____	_____
5.	_____	_____

▶ **Practice 6. Information questions with *can*.** (Chart 12-3)
Match the question with the correct answer.

1. What can I get you? _____

2. Where can I register for class? _____

3. When can we leave? _____

4. Who can they talk to about their problem? _____

5. Where can I find the hotel manager? _____

a. The manager.

b. After class.

c. In the school administration
office.

d. At the reservation desk.

e. Some coffee, please.

▶ **Practice 7. *Know how to*.** (Chart 12-4)
Rewrite the sentences using ***know how to***.

1. Toni can make pizza.

   _____*Toni knows how to make pizza.*_____

2. Martha can play chess.

   _____

3. Sonya and Thomas can speak Portuguese.

   _____

4. Jack can't speak Russian.

   _____

5. My brothers can't cook.

   _____

6. I can't change a flat tire.

   _____

7. We can't play musical instruments.

   a flat tire

   _____

8. Can you type?

   _____

9. Can your children swim?

   _____

10. Can Ari kick a soccer ball very far?

    _____

▶ **Practice 8. _Know how to._** (Chart 12-4)
  Write sentences about what you and others **_know how to_** do or **_don't_**
  know how to do. Use the words from the list or your own words.

dance	drive a stick-shift car	milk a cow
cook rice	knit	sew clothes
do advanced math	make candy	use chopsticks

  1. I _____ .

  2. I _____ .

  3. (_name of your best friend_) _____ .

  She knows how to knit.

Modals, Part 1: Expressing Ability **211**

4. My best friend and I _____ .

5. (*name of a cousin*) _____ .

6. (*name of a classmate*) _____ .

7. (*name of a classmate*) _____ .

▶ **Practice 9. Could.** (Chart 12-5)
Stefan and Heidi decided to live without electricity for one month. Write what they ***could*** and
couldn't do for that month.

✓ watch TV	spend time together	use electric heat
cook over a fire	use a computer	have heat from a fireplace
read books	turn on the lights	play board games

1. _____ *They couldn't watch TV.* _____

2. _____

3. _____

4. _____

5. _____

6. _____

7. _____

8. _____

9. _____

► **Practice 10. *Can* or *could*.** (Charts 12-1 and 12-5)
Choose the correct answer in each sentence.

1. Yesterday we (*can't / couldn't*) go to the beach. It rained all day.

2. Please turn down the music! I (*can't / couldn't*) study.

3. (*Could / Can*) you speak English a few years ago?

4. I'm a fast typist. I (*can / could*) type 90 words-per-minute on my computer.

5. Sam (*could / can*) tell time when he was four years old.

6. (*Could / Can*) you finish the math test yesterday?

7. Our neighbors (*can't / couldn't*) control their dog. She needs dog-training classes.

► **Practice 11. *Can* and *could*.** (Charts 12-1 and 12-5)
Two months ago, Arturo fell off his bike and broke his leg. He was in a cast for six weeks. Now he is okay. Write what he ***couldn't*** do two months ago and ***can*** do now. Use the appropriate phrases from the box.

> do homework   play soccer
> ✓ drive a car   ride a bike
> go swimming   talk on the phone
> listen to music   watch TV

1. Two months ago, __*he couldn't drive a car.*__   Now, __*he can drive a car.*__

2. Two months ago, _____   Now, _____

3. Two months ago, _____   Now, _____

4. Two months ago, _____   Now, _____

► **Practice 12. *Can* or *could*.** (Charts 12-1 and 12-5)
Complete the sentences with ***can*, *can't*, *could*,** or ***couldn't*.**

1. When I was a newborn baby, I _____*couldn't*_____ walk.

2. When I was a newborn baby, I _____ talk.

3. When I entered kindergarten, I _____ read and write my language.

4. A few years ago, I _____ speak a lot of English.

5. Now I _____ read and write some English.

Modals, Part 1: Expressing Ability **213**

6. I _____ understand native English speakers well.

7. I _____ always understand my English teacher.

▶ **Practice 13. _Be able to._** (Chart 12-6)
Make sentences with the present, past, and future forms of _be able to_.

	Able to (Present)	_Able to_ (Past)	_Able to_ (Future)
1. I can run.	_I am able to run._	_I was able to run._	_I will be able to run._
2. You can draw.	_____	_____	_____
3. He can drive.	_____	_____	_____
4. She can swim.	_____	_____	_____
5. We can dance.	_____	_____	_____
6. They can type.	_____	_____	_____

▶ **Practice 14. _Be able to._** (Chart 12-6)
Make sentences with the present and past forms of _be able to_.

1. When I was a newborn baby, I _____ _wasn't able to_ _____ walk.

2. When I was a newborn baby, I _____ talk.

3. When I entered kindergarten, I _____ read and write my language.

4. A few years ago, I _____ speak a lot of English.

5. Now I _____ read and write some English.

6. I _____ understand native English speakers well now.

7. I _____ understand my English teacher all the time.

▶ **Practice 15. _Be able to._** (Chart 12-6)
Choose the sentence that is closest in meaning to the given sentence.

1. James can run very fast.
   a. He will be able to run very fast.
   (b.) He is able to run very fast.
   c. He was able to run very fast.

2. I will be able to have dinner with you.
   a. I can have dinner with you.
   b. I could have dinner with you.
   c. I was able to have dinner with you.

3. Jean couldn't finish her science project.

    a. She isn't able to finish her science project.

    b. She wasn't able to finish her science project.

    c. She won't be able to finish her science project.

4. My roommate wasn't able to come to the party.

    a. He won't be able to come to the party.

    b. He can't come to the party.

    c. He couldn't come to the party.

5. I can't help you later.

    a. I wasn't able to help you.

    b. I couldn't help you.

    c. I won't be able to help you.

▶ **Practice 16.** *Be able to.* (Chart 12-6)
Rewrite the boldfaced verbs with the correct form of *be able to*.

wasn't able to speak

    Five years ago, Chang was in Australia. He **couldn't speak** any English. He had a difficult
1

time communicating. He **couldn't ask** questions. People **couldn't give** him directions.
2   3

Many times he got lost. He **couldn't visit** tourist sites he was interested in. He was frustrated
4

because he **couldn't have** conversations with people.
5

    So Chang decided to study English. Four years later, he went back to Australia. He was

surprised he **could understand** so much. People **could have** long conversations with him.
6   7

He **could learn** about local customs. He **could visit** interesting tourist areas. This time
8   9

Chang had a great trip. Learning English made a big difference.

► **Practice 17. *Can, can't, be able to*, and *know how to*.** (Chart 12-6)
Choose <u>all</u> the grammatically correct verbs.

1. Alex _____ to program computers.
   a. can
   b. is able
   c. are able
   d. know how
   e. knows how

2. Mr. and Mrs. Cox _____ fix their car.
   a. can
   b. know how to
   c. knows how to
   d. isn't able to
   e. aren't able to

3. Jerry is _____ speak several languages.
   a. able to
   b. not able to
   c. can't
   d. know how to
   e. knows how to

4. Two of my friends don't _____ swim.
   a. can't
   b. aren't able to
   c. knows how to
   d. can
   e. know how to

5. Ellen doesn't _____ create movies on a computer.
   a. knows how to
   b. know how to
   c. can
   d. able to
   e. can't

► **Practice 18. *Very or too*.** (Chart 12-7)
Complete the sentences with ***very*** or ***too***.

1. This leather coat is _____*too*_____ expensive. I can't buy it.

2. The tea is _____ hot, but I can drink it.

3. The shoe store is _____ big. There's a good selection.

4. The neighbors are _____ noisy. I want them to move.

5. These pants are _____ short. I'm not going to buy them.

6. My teacher talks _____ fast. It's good practice for me.

7. This car is _____ small. It won't use a lot of gas.

8. The Arctic Circle is _____ cold. I don't want to travel there.

▶ **Practice 19. *Very or too.*** (Chart 12-7)
Choose the best completion for each sentence.

1. Do you like this book?
   a. Yes, it's very interesting.   b. Yes, it's too interesting.

2. I can't watch this movie.
   a. It's too violent.   b. It's very violent.

3. You had no mistakes on your math test.
   a. Your knowledge of math is too good.   b. Your knowledge of math is very good.

4. We can do these math problems.
   a. They're too easy.   b. They're very easy.

5. This dress is too tight.
   a. I can't wear it.   b. I can wear it.

6. This puzzle looks very tricky.
   a. Let's see if we can figure it out.   b. It will be impossible to do.

7. Thomas is too friendly.
   a. I feel comfortable around him.   b. I feel uncomfortable around him.

8. Let's buy this mattress.
   a. It's very comfortable.   b. It's too comfortable.

▶ **Practice 20. *Very or too.*** (Chart 12-7)
Write answers to the questions.

1. What school subjects are very hard for you?

   _____

2. What school subjects are too hard for you?

   _____

3. What foods do you think are very spicy?

   _____

4. What foods are too spicy for you?

   _____

5. What cities have climates that are too hot for you?

   _____

6. What cities have climates that are too cold for you?

   _____

▶ **Practice 21. Review.** (Chapter 12)
Choose the correct completion for each sentence.

1. _____ play a musical instrument?

    a. Do you can   b. Can you   c. Do you be able to   d. Can you to

2. I _____ my homework. I was too tired.

    a. couldn't to finish   b. could finish   c. couldn't finish   d. couldn't finished

3. I don't know how _____ to the Palace Hotel from here.

    a. do I get   b. get   c. getting   d. to get

4. Gina _____ understand the speaker at the lecture last night.

    a. couldn't   b. doesn't able to   c. won't be able to   d. can't

5. My uncle can't _____ English.

    a. to speak   b. speaking   c. speaks   d. speak

6. The driving test was _____. I was so happy to pass it.

    a. very hard   b. too hard   c. very easy   d. too easy

7. Sorry, I _____ to get movie tickets. They were sold out.

    a. can't   b. didn't   c. couldn't   d. wasn't able

▶ **Practice 22. Verb review.** (Chapter 12)
Complete the sentences with the words in parentheses. Use any appropriate verb form.

Once upon a time there (be) _____ *a mouse named Young Mouse. He lived*

                                                  1
near a river with his family and friends. Every day he and the other mice did the same things.

They (hunt) _____ *for food and* (take) _____ *care*

                              2   3
of their mouse holes. In the evening they (listen) _____ *to stories around a*

                                                        4
fire. Young Mouse especially liked to listen to stories about the Far Away Land. He (dream)

_____ *about the Far Away Land. It sounded wonderful. One day he* (decide)

                        5

_____ *to go there.*

                        6

YOUNG MOUSE: Good-bye, Old Mouse. I'm leaving now.

OLD MOUSE: Why (*you, leave*) _____?

                                                7
Where (*you, go*) _____?

                            8

YOUNG MOUSE: I (*go*) _____ to a new and different place. I (*go*)

                                      9

_____ to the Far Away Land.

                          10

OLD MOUSE: Why (*you, want*) _____ (*go*) _____ there?

                                      11   12

YOUNG MOUSE: I (*want*) _____ (*experience*) _____ all

                                      13   14
of life. I (*need*) _____ (*learn*) _____ about everything.

                            15   16

OLD MOUSE: You (can learn) _____ many things if you (stay)
17
_____ here with us. Please stay here with us.
18

YOUNG MOUSE: No, I (can stay, not) _____ here by the river for the rest
19
of my life. There (be) _____ too much to learn about in the world. I must
20
go to the Far Away Land.

OLD MOUSE: The trip to the Far Away Land is a long and dangerous journey. You (have)
_____ many problems before you (get) _____ there. You
21   22
(face) _____ many dangers.
23

YOUNG MOUSE: I understand that, but I need to find out about the Far Away Land. Good-
bye, Old Mouse. Good-bye, everyone! I (may see, never) _____ any of
24
you again, but I (try) _____ to return from the Far Away Land someday.
25
Good-bye!

So Young Mouse left to fulfill his dream of going to the Far Away Land. His first problem was the
river. At the river, he met a frog.

MAGIC FROG: Hello, Young Mouse. I'm Magic Frog. (you, need) _____
26
help?

YOUNG MOUSE: Yes. How (I, can cross) _____ this river? I (know, not)
27
_____ how to swim. If I (can cross, not) _____ this river,
28   29
I (be able, not) _____ to reach the Far Away Land.
30

MAGIC FROG: I (help) _____ you to cross the river. I (give)
31
_____ you the power of my legs so you (can jump) _____
32   33
across the river. I (give, also) _____ you a new name. Your new name
34
will be Jumping Mouse.

JUMPING MOUSE: Thank you, Magic Frog.

MAGIC FROG: You are a brave mouse, Jumping
Mouse, and you have a good heart. If you (lose,
not) _____ hope, you (reach)
35
_____ the Far Away Land.
36

With his powerful new legs, Jumping Mouse jumped across the
river. He traveled fast for many days across a wide grassland. One
day he met a buffalo. The buffalo was lying on the ground.

JUMPING MOUSE: Hello, Buffalo. My name is Jumping Mouse. Why (*you, lie*★)

_____ on the ground? (*you, be*) _____ ill?
　　　　　37　　　　　　　　　　　　　　　　　　　　　　38

BUFFALO: Yes. I (*can see, not*) _____. I (*drink*) _____
　　　　　　　　　　　　　　　　　　39　　　　　　　　　　　　　　　　40

some poisoned water, and now I (*be*) _____ blind. I (*die*)
　　　　　　　　　　　　　　　　　　　　41

_____ soon because I (*can find, not*) _____ food and
　　　42　　　　　　　　　　　　　　　　　　　　　　　　43

water without my eyes.

JUMPING MOUSE: When I started my journey, Magic Frog (*give*) _____
　　　　　　　　　　　　　　　　　　　　　　　　　　　　　　　　　　44

me her powerful legs so I could jump across the river. What (*I, can give*)

_____ you to help you? I know! I (*give*) _____ you my
　　　45　　　　　　　　　　　　　　　　　　　　　　　　46

sight so you can see to find food and water.

BUFFALO: Are you really going to do that? Jumping Mouse, you are very kind! Ah!

Yes, I (*can see*) _____ again. Thank you! But now you (*can see, not*)
　　　　　　　　　　　47

_____. How (*you, find*) _____ the Far Away Land? I
　　　48　　　　　　　　　　　　　　　　　　　49

know. Jump onto my back. I (*carry*) _____ you across this land to the foot
　　　　　　　　　　　　　　　　　　　　50

of the mountain.

JUMPING MOUSE: Thank you, Buffalo.

So Jumping Mouse found a way to reach the mountain. When they reached the mountain,

Jumping Mouse and Buffalo parted.

BUFFALO: I don't live in the mountains, so I (*can go, not*) _____ any
　　　　　　　　　　　　　　　　　　　　　　　　　　　　51

farther.

JUMPING MOUSE: What (*I, do*) _____? I (*have*) _____
　　　　　　　　　　　　　　　　52　　　　　　　　　　　　　　53

powerful legs, but I can't see.

★ The *-ing* form of *lie* is spelled *lying*.

BUFFALO: Keep your hope alive. You (*find*) _____ a way to reach the Far
54

Away Land.

Jumping Mouse was very afraid. He didn't know what to do. Suddenly he heard a wolf.

JUMPING MOUSE: Hello? Wolf? I (*can see, not*) _____ you, but I
55

(*can hear*) _____ you.
56

WOLF: Yes, Jumping Mouse. I'm here, but I (*can help, not*) _____ you
57

because I (*die★*) _____.
58

JUMPING MOUSE: What's wrong? Why (*you, die*) _____?
59

WOLF: I (*lose*) _____ my sense of smell many weeks ago, so now I
60

(*can find, not*) _____ food. I (*starve*) _____ to death.
61   62

JUMPING MOUSE: Oh, Wolf, I (*can help*) _____ you. I (*give*)
63

_____ you my ability to smell.
64

WOLF: Oh, thank you, Jumping Mouse. Yes, I (*can smell*) _____ again.
65

Now I'll be able to find food. That is a wonderful gift! How (*I, can help*)

_____ you?
66

JUMPING MOUSE: I (*try*) _____ to get to the Far Away Land. I (*need*)
67

_____ (*go*) _____ to the top of the mountain.
68   69

WOLF: Come over here. I (*put*) _____ you on my back and (*take*)
70

_____ you to the top of the mountain.
71

So Wolf carried Jumping Mouse to the top of the mountain. But then Wolf left.

Jumping Mouse was all alone. He (can see, not) _____ *and he*
72

(can smell, not) _____, *but he still had powerful legs. He almost* (lose)
73

_____ *hope. Then suddenly, he* (hear) _____ *Magic Frog.*
74   75

★ The *-ing* form of *die* is spelled *dying*.

JUMPING MOUSE: Is that you, Magic Frog? Please help me. I'm all alone and afraid.

MAGIC FROG: Don't cry, Jumping Mouse. You have a generous, open heart. You (be, not) _____ selfish. You help others. Your unselfishness caused you
               76
suffering during your journey, but you (lose, never) _____ hope. Now you
                                        77
are in the Far Away Land. Jump, Jumping Mouse. Use your powerful legs to jump high in the air. Jump! Jump!

Jumping Mouse jumped as high as he could, up, up, up. He reached his arms out to his sides and started to fly. He felt strong and powerful.

JUMPING MOUSE: I can fly! I can fly! I (fly) _____!
                                            78

MAGIC FROG: Jumping Mouse, I am going to give you a new name. Now your name is Eagle!

So Jumping Mouse became the powerful Eagle and fulfilled his dream of reaching the Far Away Land and experiencing all that life has to offer.

This fable is based on a Native American story and has been adapted from *The Story of Jumping Mouse* by John Steptoe; Lothrop, Lee & Shepard books, 1984.

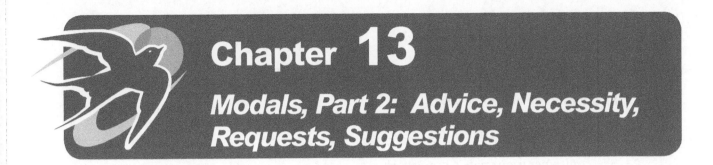

Chapter 13

Modals, Part 2: Advice, Necessity, Requests, Suggestions

▶ **Practice 1. Should.** (Chart 13-1)
Create your own chart by completing each sentence with the correct form of **should + study**.

1. Mrs. Wang _____ *should study* _____ more.

2. He _____ more.

3. We _____ more.

4. You _____ more.

5. She _____ more.

6. They _____ more.

7. I _____ more.

8. Nick and I _____ more.

9. The students _____ more.

▶ **Practice 2. Should.** (Chart 13-1)
Complete the sentences with **should** or **shouldn't**.

Sami wants to be on his high school soccer team.

1. He _____ *should* _____ practice kicking a ball with his friends.

2. He _____ exercise a lot.

3. He _____ smoke cigarettes.

4. He _____ stop doing homework so he has more time for soccer.

5. He _____ practice running fast.

6. He _____ watch famous soccer games.

7. He _____ eat a lot of snack foods.

► **Practice 3. Should.** (Chart 13-1)
Write sentences with **should** or **shouldn't**.

Rose gets failing grades in school. She wants to get better grades.

1. She doesn't do her homework.

   She should do her homework.

2. She copies her roommate's homework.

   She shouldn't copy her roommate's homework.

3. She doesn't study for her tests.

   _____

4. She stays up late.

   _____

5. She daydreams in class.

   _____

6. She is absent from class a lot.

   _____

7. She doesn't take notes during lectures.

   _____

8. She doesn't take her books to school.

   _____

► **Practice 4. Should.** (Chart 13-1)
Give advice with **should** or **shouldn't**.

1. Sara's bedroom is very messy. She can't find her clothes.

   Sara ___ *should clean her room.* ___

2. The Browns play loud music at night. It wakes up the neighbors.

   The neighbors _____

3. Janet is a dance teacher. She has a backache.

   Janet _____

4. Bill has a sore tooth. It began to hurt four weeks ago.

   Bill _____

5. Ronnie isn't careful with his money. He spends too much and he's always broke.*

   Ronnie _____

6. Mr. and Mrs. Brown are traveling to South America soon. They don't have visas.

   They _____

▶ **Practice 5. *Have to* and *has to*.** (Chart 13-2)
Create your own chart by completing each sentence with the correct form of ***have to/has to* +
*leave***.

1. I _____*have to leave*_____ soon.

2. We _____ soon.

3. They _____ soon.

4. You _____ soon.

5. He _____ soon.

6. She _____ soon.

7. My parents (not) _____ soon.

8. The children (not) _____ soon.

9. Mark (not) _____ soon.

10. Mark and I (not) _____ soon.

▶ **Practice 6. *Have to* and *has to*.** (Chart 13-2)
Complete the sentences with ***has to*** or ***doesn't have to***.

Roger wants to be a pediatrician (children's doctor). What qualities does he have to have?

1. He _____*has to*_____ be smart.

2. He _____*doesn't have to*_____ be good-looking.

3. He _____ be patient.

4. He _____ speak several languages fluently.

5. He _____ be athletic.

6. He _____ like children.

7. He _____ like working with sick people.

---

*be broke = have no money.

▶ **Practice 7. Have to and _has to_.** (Chart 13-2)
Complete each sentence with **_have to/has to_** or **_don't have to/doesn't have to_**.

1. We _____ have to _____ leave now. Our class starts soon.

2. We _____ hurry. We're almost there.

3. A good teacher _____ begin on time.

4. The students _____ arrive on time. Late students get lower grades.

5. Students _____ arrive before 8:00. The school isn't open.

6. I _____ study hard. I want to go to medical school.

7. Jane _____ take difficult science classes. She wants to be an artist.

8. Teachers _____ correct a lot of homework. They collect it every day.

9. My teacher _____ correct a lot of papers. She has 50 students.

10. My friend's teacher has five students. She _____ correct a lot of papers.

▶ **Practice 8. _Had to_ or _didn't have to_.** (Chart 13-2)
Read the information about Mr. Napoli. Then complete each sentence with **_had to_** or **_didn't have to_**.

   Mr. Napoli is retired now. For thirty years, he owned a successful bakery. His bakery opened at 5:00 A.M. and closed at 7:00 P.M. What did he have to do? What didn't he have to do?

1. He _____ had to _____ work hard.

2. He _____ get up early.

3. His home was above the bakery. He _____ take the bus to work.

4. He _____ be friendly to his customers.

5. His wife took the children to school. He _____ take them.

6. He _____ work long hours.

7. His workers did the cleaning. He _____ clean up at night.

8. He _____ begin baking before 5:00 A.M.

▶ **Practice 9. *Had to* or *didn't have to*.** (Chart 13-2)
What chores did Nina have to do last week? Complete each sentence with **had to** or **didn't
have to**.

```
┌─────────────────────────────────┐
│      ┌──────────────┐    ┌──┐    │
│      │ ══════════   │    │  │    │
│      │ Nina's Chores (4/1– 4/7)│ │  │    │
│      │   Clean bedroom│    │  │    │
│      │   Fold laundry │    │  │    │
│      │   Feed pets    │    │  │    │
│      │   Vacuum floors│    │  │    │
│      └──────────────┘    └──┘    │
└─────────────────────────────────┘
```

1. She _____ *had to* _____ clean her bedroom.

2. She _____ cook dinner for her family.

3. She _____ empty the garbage.

4. She _____ fold the laundry.

5. She _____ wash her clothes.

6. She _____ feed the pets.

7. She _____ sweep the floors.

8. She _____ vacuum the floors.

▶ **Practice 10. *Should*, *have to*, and *don't have to*.** (Charts 13-1 and 13-2)
Complete each sentence with **should**, **have to**, or **don't have to**.

High school students in my country . . .

1. _____ work hard.

2. _____ go to school on Saturdays.

3. _____ stand up when the teacher comes in the room.

4. _____ clean the classroom after class.

5. _____ do homework every day.

6. _____ take extra classes after school or in the evening.

7. _____ memorize a lot of information.

8. _____ work together in small groups.

9. _____ be polite to other students.

10. _____ bring a dictionary to class.

11. _____ wear uniforms to school.

► **Practice 11. Must or must not.** (Chart 13-3)
Complete each sentence with **must** or **must not**.

Swimming Pool Rules

1. Swimmers _____*must*_____ take a shower before entering the pool.

2. Small children _____ be with a parent.

3. Non-swimmers _____ go in the deep end of the pool.

4. Non-swimmers _____ wear lifejackets.

5. Swimmers _____ dive in the shallow* end of the pool.

6. Non-swimmers _____ jump off the diving board.

► **Practice 12. Must or must not.** (Chart 13-3)
Complete each sentence with **must** or **must not**.

Beth is going to have surgery. What is her doctor going to tell her after the surgery?

1. She _____*must*_____ take her medicine.

2. She _____ go to work the next day.

3. She _____ rest.

4. She _____ lift heavy objects for several weeks.

5. She _____ call her doctor if she gets a fever.

6. She _____ stay quiet.

shallow = opposite of deep.

▶ **Practice 13. *Must* or *should*.** (Charts 13-1 and 13-3)
Complete each sentence with *must* or *should*.

1. You _____*should*_____ make your bed every day. Your bedroom looks nicer when you make it.

2. You _____ take vitamins every day. They may help you stay healthy.

3. You _____ obey the speed limit. If you drive too fast, you will get a ticket.

4. You _____ bring your dictionary to writing class, but if you don't, you can use the teacher's.

5. If you want to go to a top university, you _____ have good grades.

6. You _____ watch old movies if you want to relax.

7. You _____ rest when you are tired.

8. You _____ stop in traffic when the light is red.

9. You _____ have an I.D. when you travel to another country.

▶ **Practice 14. *May I, Could I,* and *Can I*.** (Chart 13-4)
Make polite questions using *May I, Could I,* or *Can I please*.

1. You are at a restaurant. Your coffee is cold. You want hot coffee.

   ___*May I / Could I / Can I please have some hot coffee?*___

2. You are in class. You want to look at your classmate's dictionary for a minute.

   _____

3. You are taking a test. You want to sharpen your pencil.

   _____

4. You are stuck in traffic with your friend. You want to borrow her cell phone.

   _____

5. You are in the library. You lost your library card. You need a new one.

   _____

► **Practice 15. *Could you* and *Would you*.** (Chart 13-5)
Write polite questions with *Could you* or *Would you please*.

1. You didn't hear your teacher's question. You want him/her to repeat it.

   Could / Would you please repeat the question?

2. You are a parent. You want your teenager to clean his bedroom.

   _____

3. You are a teenager. You want your parent to give you some money for a movie.

   _____

4. You are studying at home. You want your roommate to turn down the TV.

   _____

5. You are at a restaurant. The server brings you cream for your coffee and it is sour. You want some fresh cream.

   _____

6. You are at a park with your friends. You want someone to take a picture of all of you. You ask a person nearby.

   _____

► **Practice 16. Imperative sentences.** (Chart 13-6)
Choose the actions you usually do with each given activity.

1. Writing a check:
   a. Sign your name.
   b. Date the check.
   c. Fold the check and put it away.
   d. Call the bank after you write the check.

2. Making tea:
   a. Put oil in a pan.
   b. Boil water.
   c. Put a tea bag into a cup.
   d. Cool the tea with ice cubes.

3. Before an airplane takes off:
   a. Fasten your seat belt.
   b. Enter the cockpit and talk with the pilot.
   c. Put carry-on bags under your seat or in the overhead bin.
   d. Ask the flight attendant for a meal.

► **Practice 17. Imperative sentences.** (Chart 13-6)
Underline the imperative verbs in the following conversations.

1. MICHELLE: May I come in?

   PROFESSOR: Certainly. <u>Come</u> in. How can I help you?

   MICHELLE: I need to ask you a question about yesterday's lecture.

   PROFESSOR: Okay. What's the question?

2. STUDENT: Do we have any homework for tomorrow?

   TEACHER: Yes. Read pages 24 through 36, and answer the questions on page 37, in writing.

   STUDENT: Is that all?

   TEACHER: Yes.

3. HEIDI: Please close the window, Mike. It's a little chilly in here.

   MIKE: Okay. Is there anything else I can do for you before I leave?

   HEIDI: Could you turn off the light in the kitchen?

   MIKE: No problem. Anything else?

   HEIDI: Umm, please hand me the remote control for the TV. It's over there.

   MIKE: Sure. Here.

   HEIDI: Thanks.

   MIKE: I'll stop by again tomorrow. Take care of yourself. Take good care of that broken leg.

   HEIDI: Don't worry. I will. Thanks again.

► **Practice 18. Imperative sentences.** (Chart 13-6)
Describe how to make popcorn. Put the sentences in the correct order.

Making popcorn the old-fashioned way

_____ Stop shaking the pan when the popcorn stops popping.

_____ Put the popcorn in the pan.

_____ Shake the pan.

_____ Pour the popcorn into a bowl.

_____ Cover the pan with a lid.

_____ Pour melted butter over the popcorn.

_____ Heat the oil.

__1__ Put some oil in a pan.

_____ Salt the popcorn.

_____ Enjoy your snack!

► **Practice 19. Imperative sentences.** (Chart 13-6)
Use imperative sentences to write what you should and shouldn't do at school.

✓ sit	copy	do	work	answer	✓ chew	talk

School rules

1. _____Sit_____ quietly in class.

2. _____Don't chew_____ gum in class.

3. _____ to your friends when the teacher is talking.

4. _____ your homework.

5. _____ your classmates' homework.

6. _____ hard.

7. _____ the teacher's questions.

► **Practice 20. Imperative sentences.** (Chart 13-6)
Use imperative sentences to write about what you should and shouldn't do in the computer lab.

ask	✓ show	✓ bring	follow	talk
turn off	use	play	download	

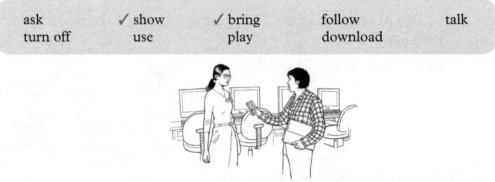

Computer lab rules at school

1. _____Show_____ your ID to the lab director when you enter the lab.

2. _____Don't bring_____ food or drinks into the computer lab.

3. _____ the lab director's instructions.

4. _____ your cell phone.

5. _____ computer games.

6. _____ the computers for school work.

7. _____ in a quiet voice.

8. _____ the lab assistant for help if you are having trouble.

9. _____ music from the Internet.

▶ **Practice 21. Modal auxiliaries.** (Chart 13-7)
Add **to** where necessary. If **to** is not necessary, write **Ø** (nothing).

1. The sky is dark. It is going _____*to*_____ rain.

2. Would you please _____ speak more slowly?

3. You should _____ meet John. He's very interesting.

4. Do we have _____ have a test tomorrow?

5. Will you _____ join us for lunch?

6. Robert might not _____ work tomorrow. He doesn't feel well.

7. I'm not able _____ help you right now.

8. The neighbors shouldn't _____ have loud parties late at night.

9. We weren't able _____ get email yesterday.

10. Monica can't _____ talk much because she has a bad cough.

▶ **Practice 22. Modal review.** (Chart 13-8)
Choose the sentence that is closest in meaning.

1. We must leave.
   a. We should leave.
   b. We have to leave.
   c. We may leave.

2. I wasn't able to come.
   a. I couldn't come.
   b. I didn't have to come.
   c. I shouldn't come.

3. Mrs. Jones will pick us up tomorrow.
   a. Mrs. Jones may pick us up.
   b. Mrs. Jones is going to pick us up.
   c. Mrs. Jones could pick us up.

4. I won't be able to meet with you tomorrow.
   a. I don't want to meet with you.
   b. I don't have to meet with you.
   c. I can't meet with you.

5. Would you close the door, please?

    a. Should you close the door?

    b. Must you close the door?

    c. Could you close the door?

6. You should take a break.

    a. You have to take a break.

    b. You might take a break.

    c. It's a good idea for you to take a break.

7. Tom didn't have to work yesterday.

    a. Tom didn't need to work.

    b. Tom couldn't work.

    c. Tom didn't want to work.

8. It might be stormy tomorrow.

    a. It must be stormy.

    b. It may be stormy.

    c. It will be stormy.

▶ **Practice 23. Let's.** (Chart 13-9)
Write a response with **Let's**.

1. A: The sun is shining. It's going to be a warm day.

    B: _____*Let's go to the park.*_____

2. A: We worked hard today.

    B: _____

3. A: Sandra's birthday is this weekend.

    B: _____

4. A: Breakfast is ready.

   B: _____

5. A: Mario's Pizzeria is having a special tonight: free pizza for kids.

   B: _____

▶ **Practice 24. Review.** (Chapter 13).
Choose the correct completion for each sentence.

1. It's very late and I have to get up early. I _____ go to bed.
   a. can   b. should   c. had to

2. We _____ up late last night. We had a lot of homework.
   a. have to stay   b. had to stayed   c. had to stay

3. It's a beautiful day. Let's _____ to the beach.
   a. going   b. to go   c. go

4. Please be quiet. I _____ the speaker very well.
   a. can't hear   b. am not hearing   c. couldn't hear

5. It's hot in here. _____ the window please?
   a. You will open   b. Could you open   c. Should you open

6. Excuse me. _____ me lift this box?
   a. Would you help   b. Would you to help   c. Would you helping

7. _____ leave now? We're having so much fun.
   a. Do we has to   b. Are we have to   c. Do we have to

8. Mia _____ pay for her groceries. She lost her wallet in the store.
   a. wasn't able   b. couldn't   c. can't to

9. The children are excited. It _____ snow tonight or tomorrow.
   a. can   b. must   c. might

10. You _____ take this medicine. You are very sick and you need it to get better.
    a. must   b. could   c. might

▶ **Practice 25. Review.** (Chapter 13)
Choose all the correct answers.

1. _____ help me carry this box?
   a. Would you
   b. Do you
   c. Could you
   d. Let's

2. Mario has a toothache. He _____ to call the dentist.

   a. have

   b. should

   c. needs

   d. must

3. Billy, you have no choice. You _____ clean your bedroom before you play with your friends.

   a. should

   b. have to

   c. had to

   d. must

4. When I was young, I _____ bend over and put my hands flat on the floor.

   a. am able

   b. could

   c. have

   d. was able to

5. It's really nice outside. _____ take a walk.

   a. We had to

   b. Let's

   c. Would we

   d. We should

6. A: Would you help me with the dishes?
   B: _____

   a. No problem.

   b. I'd be happy to.

   c. I'd be glad.

   d. Yes, of course.

7. _____ touch the pan. It's really hot.

   a. Not

   b. Don't

   c. Please

   d. Do not

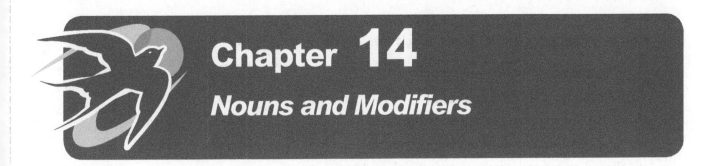

Chapter 14
Nouns and Modifiers

▶ **Practice 1. Nouns and adjectives.** (Chart 14-1)
How are the words in the box usually used? Write each word in the correct column.

✓ tall	pens	boat	true
pretty	sad	store	happy
✓ clothes	hot	horse	truth

Adjectives	**Nouns**
tall	*clothes*
_____	_____
_____	_____
_____	_____
_____	_____
_____	_____

▶ **Practice 2. Nouns and adjectives.** (Chart 14-1)
Write all the words from the box that can go before each noun. You may use a word more than once.

camera	cell	chicken
delicious	English	grammar
old	sad	tasty

1. _____ soup

2. _____ phone

3. _____ teacher

► **Practice 3. Nouns and adjectives.** (Chart 14-1)
How is the underlined word used? Circle *adjective* or *noun*.

1. The <u>camera</u> store has photography classes. (adjective)   noun
2. Do you have a digital <u>camera</u>?   adjective   noun
3. What are you going to order for <u>lunch</u>?   adjective   noun
4. Nancy's Café has a delicious <u>lunch</u> menu.   adjective   noun
5. I read an interesting <u>newspaper</u> article today about electric cars.   adjective   noun

6. Do you read the <u>newspaper</u> every day?   adjective   noun
7. We need to get some dog <u>food</u>.   adjective   noun
8. The <u>pet</u> store is having a sale.   adjective   noun

► **Practice 4. Nouns and adjectives.** (Chart 14-1)
Make two phrases for each given noun: **adjective + noun** and **noun + noun**. Use the words in the box.

accident	noisy	recipe	smelly
dangerous	old	sleeves	stairs

		Adjective + Noun	**Noun + Noun**
1.	traffic	*dangerous/noisy traffic*	*traffic accident*
2.	apartment		
3.	sandwich		
4.	shirt		

► **Practice 5. Nouns and adjectives.** (Chart 14-1)
Use the information in the first part of the sentence to complete the sentence. Use **noun + noun** in the completion.

1. A house for a dog is called a ___ *dog house* ___.

2. An article in a magazine is called a _____.

3. A card for business is called a _____.

4. An appointment with a dentist is called a _____.

5. Salad that has chicken in it is called _____.

6. A key for a house is called a _____.

7. A cord that is used with a computer is called a _____.

8. A carton for milk is called a _____.

9. A store that has clothes in it is called a _____.

10. A curtain for a shower is called a _____.

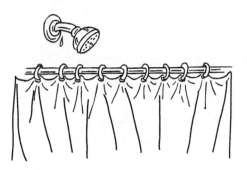

▶ **Practice 6. Nouns and adjectives.** (Chart 14-1)
Use the given words to make common **adjective + noun** or **noun + noun** phrases.

1. ***birthday***

   a. present   *birthday present*

   b. happy   *happy birthday*

   c. cake   *birthday cake*

2. ***kitchen***

   a. messy   _____

   b. cabinets   _____

   c. counter   _____

3. ***bus***

   a. city   _____

   b. schedule   _____

   c. route   _____

4. *airplane*

    a. noise   _____

    b. movie   _____

    c. ticket   _____

5. *apartment*

    a. manager   _____

    b. one-bedroom   _____

    c. building   _____

6. *phone*

    a. number   _____

    b. broken   _____

    c. call   _____

7. *patient*

    a. hospital   _____

    b. sick   _____

    c. information   _____

▶ **Practice 7. Word order of adjectives.** (Chart 14-2)
Write the words in the correct order.

1. house
   100-year-old
   small   a   *small 100-year-old house*_____

2. spicy
   food
   Mexican   some _____

3. man
   young
   kind   a _____

4. dirty
   glass
   brown   a _____

5. tall
   lovely
   rose bush   a _____

6. small   some _____
   paintings
   interesting
   old

7. film   a/an _____
   foreign
   new
   important

8. yellow   some _____
   flowers
   little

9. middle-aged   a _____
   woman
   tall

10. cabinet   a/an _____
    wooden
    Chinese
    antique

▶ **Practice 8. Word order of adjectives.** (Chart 14-2)
Choose the correct completion.

1. We work in _____ office building.
   (a.) a large old
   b. an old large

2. I spoke with a _____ man at the park today.
   a. Greek friendly
   b. friendly Greek

3. I need some _____ socks.
   a. brown comfortable
   b. comfortable brown

4. My sister makes _____ soup.
   a. vegetable delicious
   b. delicious vegetable

5. The children found _____ box at the beach.
   a. an old metal
   b. a metal old

6. My family loves _____ food.
   a. spicy Indian
   b. Indian spicy

7. Robert gave his girlfriend _____ ring.
   a. an antique beautiful
   b. a beautiful antique

8. We shared our _____ online.
   a. favorite pictures
   b. pictures favorite

9. There is a _____ soccer field near our house.
   a. wonderful big grassy*   b. grassy big wonderful

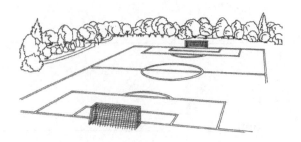

▶ **Practice 9. Linking verbs + adjectives.** (Chart 14-3)
Check (✓) the sentences that have a linking verb. <u>Underline</u> the linking verb.

1. ___✓___ After it rains, the air <u>smells</u> very fresh.
2. _____ Your vacation plans sound interesting.
3. _____ The kids are playing happily in the backyard.
4. _____ They like to run and climb trees.
5. _____ Does the vegetable soup taste good?
6. _____ The roses smell wonderful.
7. _____ They look beautiful too.
8. _____ Jack looked for some flowers for his wife.
9. _____ Cindy went to bed early because she felt sick.
10. _____ Emily seems sad. Do you know why?

▶ **Practice 10. Linking verbs + adjectives.** (Chart 14-3)
Complete each sentence with an appropriate adjective.

1. There's a new movie about space at the theater. I really want to go. It sounds
   _____*interesting*_____ .

2. Carl woke up at 3:00 A.M., and never went back to sleep. He looked
   _____ this morning.

3. Mmm. What are you baking? The kitchen smells _____ .

4. I got 100% on all my tests. I feel _____ .

5. Whew! Do you smell that smell? I think it's a skunk. It smells

   _____ .

a skunk

6. I'm sorry, this chicken tastes _____ . I can't
   eat it.

---

*grassy = covered with grass.

7. The Smiths are having a beach party this weekend. It sounds _____.
   Do you want to go?

8. A few hours after dinner, Ellen and Bill got sick. They felt _____ for
   the rest of the evening.

▶ **Practice 11. Adverbs.** (Chart 14-4)
Write the adverb forms for the given adjectives.

1.	quiet	_____*quietly*_____	8. careful	_____
2.	clear	_____	9. quick	_____
3.	neat	_____	10. slow	_____
4.	correct	_____	11. late	_____
5.	hard	_____	12. honest	_____
6.	good	_____	13. fast	_____
7.	early	_____	14. easy	_____

▶ **Practice 12. Adverbs.** (Chart 14-4)
Complete each sentence with the adverb form of the given adjective.

1. *clear*   Our teacher explains everything_____*clearly*_____.

2. *easy*   This is a simple car repair. I can do it _____.

3. *late*   Spiro came to class _____.

4. *safe*   The plane arrived at the airport _____.

5. *fast*   Mike talks too _____. I can't understand him.

6. *hard*   Ms. Chan is a hard worker. She worked _____ all her life.

7. *good*   I didn't understand my co-worker's instructions very

                _____.

8. *honest*   Andrew's reasons for missing work were hard to believe. Did you

                _____ believe them?

9. *soft*   When the students became loud, the teacher spoke _____.

10. *careless* The driver _____ threw a cigarette out the car window and
                started a forest fire.

▶ **Practice 13. Linking verbs, adjectives, and adverbs.** (Charts 14-3 and 14-4)
Complete the sentences with the adjective or adverb form of the given word. Remember, adjectives, not adverbs, follow linking verbs.

1. *nervous*   Bill looked _____ *nervous* _____.

   He began his speech _____ *nervously* _____.

   His hands shook _____ *nervously* _____.

2. *beautiful*   Rita dressed _____ for the party.

   She looked _____.

   She wears _____ clothes.

3. *good*   The flowers smell _____.

   They grow _____ in this sunny garden.

4. *good*   Does the food taste _____?

   Robert is a _____ cook.

5. *interesting* Your idea for the project sounds _____.

   The project looks _____.

6. *bad*   Anita wrote a _____ check at the store and gave it to the clerk.

   She had no money in the bank, but she didn't feel _____ about doing that.

7. *fast*   Tom drives _____.

   He speaks _____ too.

▶ **Practice 14. Adjectives and adverbs.** (Charts 14-3 and 14-4)
Complete each sentence with the adjective or adverb form of the given word.

1. *clear*   The teacher speaks _____ *clearly* _____. She gives _____ *clear* _____ examples.

2. *correct*   You answered the question _____. That is the _____ answer.

3. *late*   I paid my phone bill _____. I don't like to make _____ payments.

4. *beautiful*   Look at the _____ pictures. The artist draws

                        _____.

5. *honest*   Michael is an _____ child. He never lies. He answers

                        questions _____.

6. *handsome* Anton looked _____ on his wedding day. He is a

                        _____ man.

7. *good*   Mmm. The food smells _____. I'm glad my roommate

                        is a _____ cook.

8. *easy*   Isabelle writes _____ in English. Writing is an

                        _____ subject for her.

9. *good*   The students swam _____. The team had a

                        _____ competition.

10. *quick*   I need these copies _____. Is your copy machine

                        _____?

11. *sweet*   Candy tastes very _____. I love

                        _____ snacks.

12. *careless* John is a _____ driver. Why does he drive so

                        _____?

▶ **Practice 15. Adjective and adverb review.** (Charts 14-3 and 14-4)
Complete each sentence with the correct form of the given adjective or adverb.

1. *slow*   This is a _____*slow*_____ bus. I'm afraid we'll be late.

2. *slow*   There's a lot of traffic. The bus driver has to drive _____.

3. *hard*   The whole class studied _____ for the test.

4. *hard*   The teacher always gives _____ exams.

5. *clear*   The sky looks very _____ today.

6. *early*   The birds woke me up _____ this morning.

7. *fluent*   Jane speaks _____ French, but she can't speak English

            _____.

8. *neat*   Your homework looks very _____.

9. *careful*   It's clear that you do your work _____.

10. *good*   The teacher said our group gave a _____ presentation.

11. *good*   She said we worked together _____.

▶ **Practice 16.** *All of, most of, some of,* and *almost all of.* (Chart 14-5)
Match the picture with the sentence.

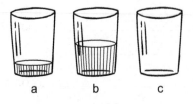

        a   b   c

  1. Meg drank most of the milk. Now the glass looks like _____*a*_____.

  2. Meg drank all of the milk. Now the glass looks like _____.

  3. Meg drank some of the milk. Now the glass looks like _____ or _____.

  4. Meg drank almost all of the milk. Now the glass looks like _____.

▶ **Practice 17. Understanding quantity expressions.** (Charts 14-5 and 14-6)
Choose the percentage that is closest in meaning to the quantity expression.

1. Almost all of the students are coming to the picnic.	(95%)	75%	100%
2. Most of the staff is coming to the picnic.	90%	100%	50%
3. All of the food for the picnic is ready.	90%	100%	95%
4. Some of the dishes are very spicy.	100%	60%	0%
5. Half of the class is bringing a friend.	50%	60%	40%
6. A lot of people in my class ride bikes to school.	75%	40%	25%
7. Some of the people in my class have motorcycles.	0%	99%	30%
8. Most of the teachers take the bus to school.	88%	65%	70%
9. All of the bus drivers are careful.	97%	90%	100%
10. Almost all of the drivers are friendly.	97%	100%	60%

▶ **Practice 18. Subject-verb agreement: expressions of quantity.** (Chart 14-6)
Choose the correct verb in each sentence.

  1. All of your English work (*is*/ *are*) correct.

  2. All of your sentences (*is* / *are*) correct.

  3. Some of your math work (*is* / *are*) correct.

  4. Almost all of your science work (*is* / *are*) correct.

  5. All of your facts (*is* / *are*) correct.

  6. Most of my classes (*is* / *are*) hard.

  7. Almost all of my classes (*is* / *are*) interesting.

  8. Almost all of the class (*is* / *are*) ready.

  9. Half of your homework (*is* / *are*) due.

  10. Half of your assigments (*is* / *are*) due.

► **Practice 19. Agreement with quantity words.** (Chart 14-6)
Complete the sentences with *is* or *are*.

1. All of the work _____*is*_____ correct.

2. All of the answers _____ correct.

3. All of the information _____ correct.

4. All of the facts _____ correct.

5. Some of your homework _____ incorrect.

6. Some of the students _____ ready.

7. Almost all of the children _____ tired.

8. A lot of the class _____ tired.

9. A lot of the students _____ tired.

10. Half of the vocabulary _____ new for me.

11. Half of the words _____ new for me.

12. Most of the food _____ gone.

13. Some of the food _____ cold.

14. All of the apples _____ from our apple tree.

15. Almost all of the fruit _____ organic.

16. Most of the vegetables _____ fresh.

► **Practice 20. Review: expressions of quantity.** (Charts 14-5 and 14-6)
Choose the correct sentence in each group.

1. a. Some of the book are hard.
   b. Some of book is hard.
   c. Some of the book is hard.

2. a. Some of the money is gone.
   b. Some of money is gone.
   c. Some of the money are gone.

3. a. All of men have hats.
   b. All of the men have hats.
   c. All of the men has hats.

4. a. Most of the chairs is empty.
   b. Most of the chairs are empty.
   c. Most of chairs are empty.

5. a. Almost all of people are late.
   b. Almost all of the people are late.
   c. Almost all of the people is late.

6. a. Half of class is from Asia.
   b. Half of the class are from Asia.
   c. Half of the class is from Asia.

7. a. Half of the hotel rooms are ready.
   b. Half of hotel rooms are ready.
   c. Half of the hotel rooms is ready.

▶ **Practice 21. Subject-verb agreement with *every* and *all*.** (Chart 14-7)
Choose the correct completion for each sentence.

1. All of the _____ are ready to graduate.
   a. student   (b.) students

2. Every _____ in this room has worked hard.
   a. person   b. people

3. All of the _____ in the store are for sale.
   a. shirt   b. shirts

4. Are all of the _____ on sale too?
   a. sweater   b. sweaters

5. Every _____ at this party likes to dance.
   a. teenager   b. teenagers

6. Do all _____ like to dance?
   a. teenager   b. teenagers

7. Every _____ in the world wants loving parents.
   a. child   b. children

8. Do all _____ want to have children?
   a. parent   b. parents

▶ **Practice 22. Subject-verb agreement with *every* and *all*.** (Chart 14-7)
Choose the correct completion for each sentence.

1. All of the teachers _____ tests every week.
   a. gives   (b.) give

2. Everyone at this school _____ hard.
   a. studies   b. study

3. ____ all of the students in your class participate in discussions?
   a. Does   b. Do

4. ____ everyone in your class participate in discussions?
   a. Does   b. Do

5. Not everybody in the class ____ to give their opinion.
   a. likes   b. like

6. All of the people in line ____ concert tickets.
   a. is buying   b. are buying

7. Everything in these rooms ____ from South America.
   a. is   b. are

8. Every child at the party ____ a present to take home.
   a. get   b. gets

9. ____ everything look okay?
   a. Does   b. Do

10. Everything ____ okay.
    a. looks   b. look

▶ **Practice 23. Subject-verb agreement with *every* and *all*.** (Chart 14-7)
Check (✓) the incorrect sentences and correct them.

1. __✓__ Every ~~of the~~ teacher~~s~~ is on time.

2. _____ Every students is on time too.

3. _____ Everything in this room is very clean.

4. _____ Everything in the kitchen sink are dirty.

5. _____ Where does all of your friends live?

6. _____ Where was everyone when I called last night?

7. _____ Everybody in my family like dessert after dinner.

8. _____ Do everyone in your family likes dessert?

9. _____ Was everybody from your office at the wedding?

10. _____ Was all of the people at the wedding your friends?

11. _____ There are ten families in my apartment building. Everyone are friendly.

12. _____ Everything is okay.

▶ **Practice 24. Indefinite pronouns.** (Chart 14-8)
Complete the sentences with **_something_**, **_someone_**, **_somebody_**, **_anything_**, **_anyone_**, or **_anybody_**.

Statement	**Negative**

1. He ate _____ *something* _____. He didn't eat _____.

2. She met _____ / _____. She didn't meet _*anyone*_ / _*anybody*_.

Question

3. Did he eat _____ / _____?

4. Did she meet _____ / _____ / _____ / _____?

Statement	**Negative**

5. They bought _____. They didn't buy _____.

6. They spoke to _____ / _____. They didn't speak to _____ / _____.

Question

7. Did they buy _____ / _____?

8. Did they speak to _____ / _____ / _____ / _____?

▶ **Practice 25. Indefinite pronouns.** (Chart 14-8)
Choose all of the correct completions.

1. Did you talk to _____ at the pharmacy?
   a. somebody
   b. anything
   c. someone
   d. anyone
   e. anybody
   f. something

2. Did you see _____ outside?
   a. somebody
   b. anything
   c. someone
   d. anyone
   e. anybody
   f. something

Pharmacy

3. I dropped off _____ at the airport.
   a. somebody
   b. anything
   c. someone
   d. anyone
   e. anybody
   f. something

4. Did you buy _____ at the mall?
   a. somebody
   b. anything
   c. someone
   d. anyone
   e. anybody
   f. something

► **Practice 26. Indefinite pronouns.** (Chart 14-8)
Complete the sentences with *something*, *someone*, *somebody*, *anything*, *anyone*, or *anybody*. Use any word that fits.

1. I didn't buy _____anything_____ on sale at the grocery store.

2. I didn't talk to _____ at the grocery store.

3. I bought _____ for you at the mall.

4. I met _____ from high school at the train station.

5. Did you learn _____ at school today?

6. Did you know _____ at the party?

7. A: Close your eyes. I have _____
      special for you.

   B: Oh, no! I forgot it was our anniversary. I don't
      have _____ for you.

8. A: Did the doctor give you _____
      for your headaches?

   B: He did some tests. He didn't give me
      _____ yet.

9. A: I need to talk to _____ about my work schedule. Are you going to
      speak with _____ too?

   B: No, I'm not going to talk to _____.

10. A: I didn't see _____ from school on the bus today.

    B: A lot of people are absent. _____ got a cold, and now half of the
       class is sick.

11. A: Did you pick up _____ for dinner tonight?

    B: Sorry, I forgot. I didn't pick up _____.

12. A: I hear a loud noise. Maybe _____ is in the garage.

    B: I didn't hear _____. Are you sure?

    A: I'll look. Hmm. I don't see _____ or _____.

Chapter 15
Making Comparisons

▶ **Practice 1. Comparative form.** (Chart 15-1)
Write the comparative form for each adjective.

1. young   *younger than* _____
2. wide   _____
3. cheap   _____
4. dark   _____
5. smart   _____
6. old   _____
7. happy   _____
8. important   _____
9. difficult   _____
10. expensive   _____
11. easy   _____
12. funny   _____
13. good   _____
14. far   _____
15. fat   _____
16. hot   _____
17. thin   _____
18. bad   _____
19. pretty   _____
20. famous   _____

▶ **Practice 2. Comparatives.** (Chart 15-1)

Complete the sentences. Use the comparative form of the given words.

1. *warm*   The weather today is _____*warmer than*_____ it was yesterday.

2. *funny*   This story is _____ that story.

3. *interesting* This book is _____ that book.

4. *smart*   Joe is _____ his brother.

5. *wide*   A highway is _____ an alley.

6. *large*   Your apartment is _____ mine.

7. *dark*   Ravi's hair is _____ Olaf's.

8. *good*   My wife's cooking is _____ mine.

9. *bad*   My cooking is _____ my wife's.

10. *confusing*   This story is _____ that story.

11. *far*   My house is _____ from downtown _____ your house is.

12. *good*   TV shows are _____ TV commercials.

13. *easy*   My English class is _____ my history class.

14. *beautiful*   A flower is _____ a weed.

a flower

a weed

▶ **Practice 3. Comparatives.** (Chart 15-1)

Compare the three places. Write comparative sentences using the given words. Give your own opinion.

the country   the city   the suburbs

Life in the . . .

1. *quiet*

_____*Life in the country is quieter than life in the city.*_____

2. *expensive*

_____

3. *relaxing*

_____

4. *busy*

_____

5. *convenient*

_____

6. *beautiful*

_____

7. *cheap*

_____

8. *nice*

_____

9. *safe*

_____

10. *good*

_____

▶ **Practice 4. Comparatives.** (Chart 15-1)
Compare the two culture classes using the given words. Give your own opinions.

Student Rating	
Culture 101 A	★★★★★
Culture 101 B	★★

CULTURE COURSES

Classes	101 A	101 B
Teaching style	discussions/games/movies	lecture
Student rating*	5/5	2/5
Homework	3 times/week	every day
Tests	3/term	every week
Average student grade	90%	75%

_____

*rating = 5 (excellent); 1 (bad).

1. *interesting* <u>101 A is more interesting than 101 B.</u>

2. *boring* _____

3. *hard* _____

4. *easy* _____

5. *popular* _____

6. *difficult* _____

7. *enjoyable* _____

▶ **Practice 5. Comparative and superlative forms.** (Charts 15-1 and 15-2)
Write both the comparative form and superlative form of the given words.

	Comparative	**Superlative**
1. expensive	*more expensive than*	*the most expensive*
2. lazy		
3. clean		
4. old		
5. young		
6. new		
7. beautiful		
8. exciting		
9. nice		
10. quiet		
11. bad		
12. fat		
13. thin		
14. hot		
15. good		
16. cheap		
17. far		

► **Practice 6. Superlatives.** (Chart 15-2)
Complete the sentences using superlatives. Give your opinion.

1. *hard subject in high school*

   The _____ *hardest subject in high school is calculus.* _____

2. *beautiful city in the world*

   The _____

3. *interesting show on TV*

   The _____

4. *boring sport to watch*

   The _____

5. *easy language to learn*

   The _____

6. *talented movie star*

   The _____

7. *relaxing place to go for vacation*

   The _____

8. *good place to live*

   The _____

► **Practice 7. Superlatives.** (Chart 15-2)
Compare the three places to eat. Use the words from the box. Write superlative sentences using the given words. Give your own opinion.

a fast-food restaurant
a 5-star restaurant
an Internet café

1. *expensive* _____ *A 5-star restaurant is the most expensive.* _____

2. *convenient* _____

3. *relaxing* _____

4. busy _____

5. nice _____

6. interesting _____

7. popular _____

8. quiet _____

9. cheap _____

10. useful _____

▶ **Practice 8. Review: comparatives and superlatives.** (Charts 15-1 and 15-2)
Write sentences using comparatives and superlatives. Use the given information.

Fluffy	Rex	Polly
15 lbs/7 kilos	70 lbs/32 kilos	1 ounce/.03 kilos
likes to sleep all day	likes to chase birds and hunt	likes to sing and look around
black and white fur	brown fur	blue and yellow feathers
2 years old	7 years old	10 years old

1. lazy _____ *Fluffy is the laziest.* _____

_____ *Fluffy is lazier than Rex.* _____

2. active _____

_____

3. young _____

_____

4. heavy _____

_____

5. colorful _____

_____

6. *big* _____

_____

7. *old* _____

_____

8. *small* _____

_____

9. *light** _____

_____

▶ **Practice 9. *One of* + superlative + plural noun.** (Chart 15-3)
Complete each sentence with the correct form of the given adjective and noun.

1. *hot \ month*   August is one of _____*the hottest months*_____ in my
hometown.

2. *fast \ car*   A Ferrari is one of _____ in the
world.

3. *happy \ family*   Sam and Mia have one of _____
in our neighborhood.

4. *funny \ child*   Ricky is one of _____ in my class.

5. *good \ manager*   Louisa Hoff is one of _____ in
our office.

6. *tall \ woman*   Donna is one of _____ in our
class.

7. *old \ man*   Ken is one of _____ in our class.

8. *interesting \ person* Dan is one of _____ in our office.

9. *scary \ animal*   A tiger is one of _____ in the
world.

10. *easy \ language*   Is English one of _____ or one of
hard \ language   _____ to learn?

---

*light = opposite of *heavy*.

► **Practice 10. *One of* + superlative + plural noun.** (Chart 15-3)
Make sentences with ***one of* + superlative**. Use the given adjectives and the sports from the box. Give your own opinion.

baseball	golf	running	skydiving	swimming
boxing	karate	skiing	soccer	walking

1. *easy sport to learn*   <u>Running is one of the easiest sports to learn.</u>

2. *dangerous* _____

3. *expensive* _____

4. *safe* _____

5. *difficult* _____

6. *interesting* _____

7. *good sport for your heart* _____

► **Practice 11. *One of* + superlative.** (Chart 15-3)
Make sentences with ***one of* + superlative**. Use the given words. Give your own opinion.

1. *small \ country*

   <u>Liechtenstein is one of the smallest countries</u> _____ in the world.

2. *big \ city*

   _____.

3. *hard \ language to learn*

   _____.

4. *interesting \ place to visit*

   _____.

5. *pretty \ place to visit*

_____.

6. *expensive \ city*

_____ to visit.

7. *important \ person*

_____ in the world.

▶ **Practice 12. Review: comparatives, superlatives, and *one of*.**
   (Charts 15-1 → 15-3)
Complete the sentences with the correct form of the given words.

1. *big*   Asia is _____ *the biggest* _____ continent in the world.

2. *big*   North America is _____ South America.

3. *hot \ place*   The Sahara Desert is one of _____ in the
                      world.

4. *cold \ place*   The Arctic Circle is one of _____ in the
                      world.

5. *long*   The Nile is _____ the Amazon.

6. *large*   Is Canada _____ than
                      Russia?

7. *large*   Russia is _____ country
                      in the world.

8. *long*   The femur (thigh bone) is
                      _____ bone in our body.

9. *small*   _____ bone in our body
                      is in the ear. It is called the stirrup bone.

10. scary   Is a crocodile _____ an alligator, or are they
                      equally scary?

11. *scary*   What do you think is _____ animal in the
                      world?

12. *dangerous \ animal* The hippopotamus is one of _____ in the
                      world.

13. *expensive \ city*   One of the _____ in the world is Tokyo.

14. *expensive*   Is Tokyo _____ than London?

► **Practice 13. Comparisons with adverbs.** (Charts 15-4 and 14-4)
Write the correct forms for the given adjectives.

	Adjective	Adverb	Comparative	Superlative
1.	quick	_quickly_	_more quickly_	_the most quickly_
2.	clear			
3.	slow			
4.	beautiful			
5.	neat			
6.	careful			
7.	fluent			
8.	good			
9.	hard			
10.	early			
11.	late			
12.	fast			

► **Practice 14. Adverbs: comparatives and superlatives.** (Chart 15-4)
Complete the sentences with the correct form (comparative or superlative) of the given adverbs.

1. *beautifully*   The art students draw _____ _more beautifully than_ _____ their instructor.

2. *carefully*   Rob drives _____ his brother.

3. *quickly*   Ted finished the test _____ of all.

4. *hard*   Who works _____ in your class?

5. *late*   The bride arrived at her wedding _____ the guests.

6. *early*   The groom arrived _____ of all.

7. *good*   Tina can swim _____ Tom.

8. *quickly*   Ana learns math _____ her classmates.

9. *slowly*   My grandfather walks _____ my grandmother.

10. *fluently*   Ben speaks English _____ of all the students.

11. *fast*   Ben learns languages _____ his classmates.

12. *good*   Sam can dive _____ of all.

▶ **Practice 15. Adjectives and adverbs: comparatives and superlatives.**
       (Charts 15-1, 15-2, 15-4, and 14-4)
Write the correct form of the given adjectives.

1. *heavy*   This suitcase is _____*heavier than*_____ that one.

2. *dangerous*   A motorcycle is _____ a bike.

3. *dangerous*   Tom drives _____ Fred.

4. *dangerous*   Steven drives _____ of all.

5. *clear*   Pedro speaks _____ Ernesto.

6. *clear*   Our reading teacher is _____ our grammar teacher.

7. *clear*   She speaks _____ of all.

8. *hard*   Nina works _____ Ivan.

9. *hard*   Carlos works _____ of all.

10. *good*   My son can play the guitar _____ I can.

11. *good*   My mother can play the guitar _____ of all.

12. *good*   I like the guitar _____ the piano.

13. *long*   My husband's workdays are _____ his co-workers' workdays.

14. *long*   His workdays are _____ of all.

15. *neat*   Mrs. Bell's handwriting looks _____
                  Mr. Bell.

16. *neat*   Mrs. Bell dresses _____
                  Mr. Bell.

► **Practice 16.** *The same (as), similar (to),* and *different (from).* (Chart 15-5)
Complete the sentences with the correct preposition (*to, as, from*) or Ø.

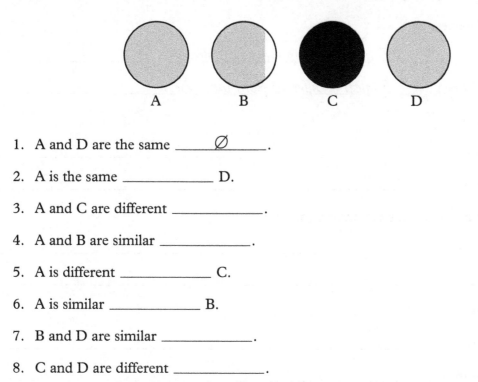

A   B   C   D

1. A and D are the same _____Ø_____.

2. A is the same _____ D.

3. A and C are different _____.

4. A and B are similar _____.

5. A is different _____ C.

6. A is similar _____ B.

7. B and D are similar _____.

8. C and D are different _____.

► **Practice 17.** *The same (as), similar (to),* and *different (from).* (Chart 15-5)
Complete the sentences using *the same (as), similar (to),* or *different (from).*

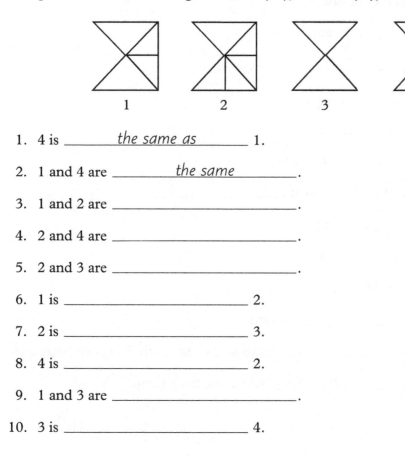

1   2   3   4

1. 4 is _____*the same as*_____ 1.

2. 1 and 4 are _____*the same*_____.

3. 1 and 2 are _____.

4. 2 and 4 are _____.

5. 2 and 3 are _____.

6. 1 is _____ 2.

7. 2 is _____ 3.

8. 4 is _____ 2.

9. 1 and 3 are _____.

10. 3 is _____ 4.

▶ **Practice 18. *The same (as), similar (to),* and *different (from).*** (Chart 15-5)
Make sentences using the given words.

1. English \ Japanese

    a. (*different*)   _____English and Japanese are different._____

    b. (*different from*)   _____English is different from Japanese._____

2. trains \ buses

    a. (*similar*)   _____

    b. (*similar to*)   _____

3. your grammar book \ my grammar book

    a. (*the same as*)   _____

    b. (*the same*)   _____

4. women \ men

    a. (*different*)   _____

    b. (*different from*) _____

▶ **Practice 19. *Like* and *alike.*** (Chart 15-6)
Complete the sentences with *like* or *alike*.

1. A pen is _____*like*_____ a pencil.

2. Fingers and toes are _____.

3. Hands and feet are _____.

4. Highways and freeways are _____.

5. A freeway is _____ a highway.

6. The Pacific Ocean and Atlantic Ocean are _____.

7. A mouse is _____ a rat.

8. A mouse isn't _____ a lion.

9. Are people around the world _____?

10. Are lakes and rivers _____ oceans?

11. French and Italian are _____ because they are both Romance languages.

12. French is _____ Italian. They both come from Latin.

► **Practice 20. *Like* and *alike*.** (Chart 15-6)
Complete the sentences with *like* or *alike* and a word from the box. Then explain why they are alike.

dark chocolate	milkshakes	physics
✓ doctors	newspapers	Thailand
knives		

1. *like*   Nurses _____ *are like doctors. They help people.* _____

2. *alike*   White chocolate _____

3. *like*   Magazines _____

4. *alike*   Scissors _____

5. *alike*   Malaysia _____

6. *like*   Ice-cream cones _____

7. *alike*   Chemistry _____

► **Practice 21. *The same as, similar (to), different (from), like*, and *alike*.**
        (Charts 15-5 and 15-6)
Choose all the completions that are grammatically correct and make sense.

1. Chapter 1 and Chapter 15 of this book are _____.
   a. different
   b. different from
   c. similar to
   d. like
   e. not the same

2. The color red is _____ the color orange.
   a. alike
   b. similar to
   c. similar
   d. like
   e. the same as

3. Lemons and limes taste _____.
   a. the same
   b. different
   c. different from
   d. alike
   e. similar

▶ **Practice 22. Review.** (Charts 15-1 → 15-6)
Part I. Read the story.

A Career Change

Martina is in college, but she is older than the other students. In fact, she is the oldest student in the class. This is her second time in college. The first time she went to college, she studied accounting. Now she is back in school because she wants to change careers.

She is interested in two fields: medicine and fire fighting. Martina likes to help people. Her mother was a nurse, and Martina learned a lot about taking care of people from her mother. Her brother is a firefighter, and she loves to hear stories about his work. She is thinking about three different careers: emergency room doctor, paramedic, or firefighter.

Martina wants an exciting job because she gets bored easily. She likes adventure and physical work. Firefighters have physically hard jobs. The work is also very dangerous. Martina likes the idea of going into burning buildings to rescue people. Of the three jobs, Martina thinks firefighting will be the most exciting.

Paramedic and emergency room work are similar. Both paramedics and doctors treat people in emergency situations. But Martina will need to spend much more time in school if she wants to be a doctor. If she chooses to become a paramedic, she can finish her studies more quickly.

The cost of education is important to her. The training for a doctor is the most expensive of the three careers. She will need scholarships or loans to pay for her education. Right now she has enough money for paramedic or firefighter training. But she knows she will earn more money later as a doctor.

She's not sure which job is the best for her. She knows she wants to help people, and she wants to do something exciting, so she is sure that she will choose one of these careers.

Part II. Check (✓) the true statements, according to the information in the story.

1. _____ The training for a paramedic is more expensive than the training for a doctor.

2. _____ Martina can become a paramedic more quickly than she can become a doctor.

3. _____ Firefighter training is cheaper than training for a doctor.

4. _____ An emergency room doctor works harder than a paramedic.

5. _____ The most exciting job for Martina will be firefighting.

6. _____ Doctors and paramedics do exactly the same work.

► **Practice 23. Using *but*.** (Chart 15-7)
Complete each sentence with the opposite adjective.

1. A sports car is fast, but a bike is _____*slow*_____.

2. The sun is hot, but the moon is _____.

3. Mr. Benton is an easy teacher, but Mrs. Benton is a _____ teacher.

4. Building a paper airplane is simple, but building a real airplane is

    _____.

5. A giraffe has a long neck, but a rabbit has a _____ neck.

6. Real diamonds are expensive, but fake diamonds are _____.

7. A hard pillow is uncomfortable, but a soft pillow is _____.

8. Red is a warm color, but blue is a _____ color.

9. Feathers are light, but rocks are _____.

10. The wheel is an old invention, but the car is a _____ invention.

► **Practice 24. Verbs after *but*.** (Chart 15-8)
Complete each sentence with an appropriate verb: affirmative or negative.

1. Fried foods are greasy, but boiled foods _____*aren't*_____.

2. Cars can't fly, but planes _____.

3. Kids often don't like vegetables, but adults generally _____.

4. Warm baths feel relaxing, but cold baths _____.

5. A warm bath feels relaxing, but a cold bath _____.

6. The students were in class yesterday, but their teacher _____.

7. Susan won't be at the party, but her husband _____.

8. I don't like fish, but my husband _____.

9. Ralph studied hard, but Daniel _____.

10. Newborn babies sleep most of the day, but adults usually _____.

11. Billy isn't a hard worker, but his brother _____.

12. A few students in the class can understand the math problems, but I _____.

13. Dr. Jones will work this weekend, but his partner _____.

14. The English books aren't in the bookstore, but the science books _____.

15. Mark wasn't on time for class, but Gary _____.

16. Mark didn't arrive on time, but Gary _____.

17. Electric cars are quiet, but diesel cars _____.

▶ **Practice 25. Verbs after *but*.** (Chart 15-8)
Complete the sentences with your own words.

1. Birds have wings, but _____*cows don't*_____.

2. Dogs bark, but _____.

3. Fish can stay underwater for a long time, but _____.

4. Skunks don't smell good, but _____.

5. The weather in the desert is hot, but _____.

6. Tight shoes aren't comfortable, but _____.

7. Honey is sweet, but _____.

8. It (was/wasn't) cold yesterday, but today it _____.

9. I will be here tomorrow, but Evan _____.

10. The Smiths are going to celebrate their anniversary, but we _____.

▶ **Practice 26. Review.** (Chapter 15)
Choose the correct completion for each sentence.

1. Fingers and toes are _____.
   (a.) similar   b. like   c. the same   d. different from

2. The weather in Canada is _____ the weather in Mexico.
   a. coolest   b. cooler than   c. the coolest   d. more cool than

3. What is your _____ color?
   a. more favorite   b. the most favorite   c. favorite   d. more favorite than

4. Men are _____ women.
   a. different from   b. different as   c. different   d. different to

5. We live _____ from town than you do.
   a. far   b. more far   c. farthest   d. farther

6. Is happiness _____ money?
   a. importanter than   c. important
   b. more important than   d. more important

7. The weather is cold today, but yesterday it _____.
    a. isn't   b. doesn't   c. wasn't   d. didn't

8. I have _____ you.
    a. a same shirt   b. same shirt   c. the same shirt as d. same shirt as

9. The Atlantic Ocean isn't _____ ocean in the world.
    a. a biggest   b. the biggest   c. a big   d. bigger than

10. Alison and Jeff don't study in the library, but Kathy _____.
    a. does   b. doesn't   c. isn't   d. is

11. I thought the math test was hard, but my friends thought it was _____.
    a. easy   b. difficult   c. easier   d. hardest

12. I thought it was one of _____ of the year.
    a. the hard test   b. a hard tests   c. a hard test   d. the hardest tests

Appendix 1
Irregular Verbs

SIMPLE FORM	SIMPLE PAST	SIMPLE FORM	SIMPLE PAST
be	was, were	keep	kept
become	became	know	knew
begin	began	leave	left
bend	bent	lend	lent
bite	bit	lose	lost
blow	blew	make	made
break	broke	meet	met
bring	brought	pay	paid
build	built	put	put
buy	bought	read	read
catch	caught	ride	rode
choose	chose	ring	rang
come	came	run	ran
cost	cost	say	said
cut	cut	see	saw
do	did	sell	sold
draw	drew	send	sent
drink	drank	shake	shook
drive	drove	shut	shut
eat	ate	sing	sang
fall	fell	sit	sat
feed	fed	sleep	slept
feel	felt	speak	spoke
fight	fought	spend	spent
find	found	stand	stood
fly	flew	steal	stole
forget	forgot	swim	swam
get	got	take	took
give	gave	teach	taught
go	went	tear	tore
grow	grew	tell	told
hang	hung	think	thought
have	had	throw	threw
hear	heard	understand	understood
hide	hid	wake up	woke up
hit	hit	wear	wore
hold	held	win	won
hurt	hurt	write	wrote

English Handwriting	
PRINTING	CURSIVE

PRINTING

Aa	Jj	Ss
Bb	Kk	Tt
Cc	Ll	Uu
Dd	Mm	Vv
Ee	Nn	Ww
Ff	Oo	Xx
Gg	Pp	Yy
Hh	Qq	Zz
Ii	Rr	

CURSIVE

Aa	Jj	Ss
Bb	Kk	Tt
Cc	Ll	Uu
Dd	Mm	Vv
Ee	Nn	Ww
Ff	Oo	Xx
Gg	Pp	Yy
Hh	Qq	Zz
Ii	Rr	

Vowels = *a, e, i, o, u*
Consonants = *b, c, d, f, g, h, j, k, l, m, n, p, q, r, s, t, v, w, x, y, z*★

★The letter *z* is pronounced "zee" in American English and "zed" in British English.

Appendix 3
Numbers

CARDINAL NUMBERS			ORDINAL NUMBERS		
1	one		1st	first	
2	two		2nd	second	
3	three		3rd	third	
4	four		4th	fourth	
5	five		5th	fifth	
6	six		6th	sixth	
7	seven		7th	seventh	
8	eight		8th	eighth	
9	nine		9th	ninth	
10	ten		10th	tenth	
11	eleven		11th	eleventh	
12	twelve		12th	twelfth	
13	thirteen		13th	thirteenth	
14	fourteen		14th	fourteenth	
15	fifteen		15th	fifteenth	
16	sixteen		16th	sixteenth	
17	seventeen		17th	seventeenth	
18	eighteen		18th	eighteenth	
19	nineteen		19th	nineteenth	
20	twenty		20th	twentieth	
21	twenty-one		21st	twenty-first	
22	twenty-two		22nd	twenty-second	
23	twenty-three		23rd	twenty-third	
24	twenty-four		24th	twenty-fourth	
25	twenty-five		25th	twenty-fifth	
26	twenty-six		26th	twenty-sixth	
27	twenty-seven		27th	twenty-seventh	
28	twenty-eight		28th	twenty-eighth	
29	twenty-nine		29th	twenty-ninth	
30	thirty		30th	thirtieth	
40	forty		40th	fortieth	
50	fifty		50th	fiftieth	
60	sixty		60th	sixtieth	
70	seventy		70th	seventieth	
80	eighty		80th	eightieth	
90	ninety		90th	ninetieth	
100	one hundred		100th	one hundredth	
200	two hundred		200th	two hundredth	
1,000	one thousand		1,000th	one thousandth	
10,000	ten thousand		10,000th	ten thousandth	
100,000	one hundred thousand		100,000th	one hundred thousandth	
1,000,000	one million		1,000,000th	one millionth	

Appendix 4

Days/Months/Seasons

DAYS	ABBREVIATION	MONTHS	ABBREVIATION	SEASONS*
Monday	Mon.	January	Jan.	winter
Tuesday	Tues.	February	Feb.	spring
Wednesday	Wed.	March	Mar.	summer
Thursday	Thurs.	April	Apr.	fall or autumn
Friday	Fri.	May	May	
Saturday	Sat.	June	Jun.	
Sunday	Sun.	July	Jul.	
		August	Aug.	
		September	Sept.	
		October	Oct.	
		November	Nov.	
		December	Dec.	

*Seasons of the year are only capitalized when they begin a sentence.

WRITING DATES:

Month/Day/Year

10/31/41	=	October 31, 1941
4/15/98	=	April 15, 1998
7/4/1906	=	July 4, 1906
7/4/07	=	July 4, 2007

SAYING DATES:

Usual Written Form	Usual Spoken Form
January 1	January first / the first of January
March 2	March second / the second of March
May 3	May third / the third of May
June 4	June fourth / the fourth of June
August 5	August fifth / the fifth of August
October 10	October tenth / the tenth of October
November 27	November twenty-seventh / the twenty-seventh of November

Appendix 5
Two-Syllable Verbs: Spelling of -ED and -ING

	VERB	SPEAKING STRESS		Some verbs have two syllables. In (a): *visit* has two syllables: *vis + it*. In the word *visit*, the stress is on the first syllable. In (b): the stress is on the second syllable in the word *admit*.
(a)	visit	**VIS** • it		
(b)	admit	ad • **MIT**		

	VERB	STRESS	*-ED* FORM	*-ING* FORM	For two-syllable verbs that end in a vowel and a consonant:
(c)	visit	**VIS** • it	visited	visiting	• The consonant is not doubled if the stress is on the first syllable, as in (c) and (d).
(d)	open	**O** • pen	opened	opening	
(e)	admit	ad • **MIT**	admitted	admitting	• The consonant is doubled if the stress is on the second syllable, as in (e) and (f).
(f)	occur	oc • **CUR**	occurred	occurring	

<table>
<tr><td colspan="8" align="center">COMMON VERBS</td></tr>
<tr><td colspan="4">Stress on first syllable:</td><td colspan="4">Stress on second syllable:</td></tr>
<tr><td>VERB</td><td>STRESS</td><td>-ED FORM</td><td>-ING FORM</td><td>VERB</td><td>STRESS</td><td>-ED FORM</td><td>-ING FORM</td></tr>
<tr><td>answer</td><td>AN • swer</td><td>answered</td><td>answering</td><td>prefer</td><td>pre • FER</td><td>preferred</td><td>preferring</td></tr>
<tr><td>happen</td><td>HAP • pen</td><td>happened</td><td>happening</td><td>permit</td><td>per • MIT</td><td>permitted</td><td>permitting</td></tr>
<tr><td>listen</td><td>LIS • ten</td><td>listened</td><td>listening</td><td>refer</td><td>re • FER</td><td>referred</td><td>referring</td></tr>
<tr><td>offer</td><td>OF • fer</td><td>offered</td><td>offering</td><td>begin</td><td>be • GIN</td><td>(no -ed form)</td><td>beginning</td></tr>
<tr><td>enter</td><td>EN • ter</td><td>entered</td><td>entering</td><td></td><td></td><td></td><td></td></tr>
</table>

Index

Answer Key

CHAPTER 9

PRACTICE 1, p. 144.
2. A: When did he leave?
   B: He left on March 22.
3. A: Why did he go there?
   B: He went to visit family.
4. A: Where did Serena go?
   B: She went to the Canary Islands.
5. A: When/What time did she leave?
   B: She left at 6 AM.
6. A: Why did she go there?
   B: She went there for vacation.

PRACTICE 2, p. 145.
2. f
3. e
4. c
5. d
6. a

PRACTICE 3, p. 145.
2. When/What time did you leave the library?
3. Why did you leave the library?
4. Where did your friends and you go yesterday afternoon?
5. When did Sandra get back from Brazil?
6. Why was Bobby in bed?
7. Why was Bobby sick?
8. Where did you buy your sandals?

PRACTICE 4, p. 146.
2. Why didn't you ask the teacher?
3. Why didn't you bring the homework?
4. Why didn't you tell me the truth?
5. Why didn't you go to Sharon's party?
6. Why didn't you clean your bedroom?

PRACTICE 5, p. 146.
3. What did you study?
4. Did you study math?
5. What are they looking at?
6. Are they looking at a map?
7. What did you dream about last night?
8. Is she a new employee?
9. What does she tutor?
10. What did David talk about?
11. Did David talk about his country?
12. What are you thinking about?
13. What does *nothing in particular* mean?
14. What are you afraid of?

PRACTICE 6, p. 147.
2. a. Lea?
   b. the nurse check?
3. a. Felix help?
   b. the new assistant? Felix.
4. a. the advanced students?
   b. Professor Jones teach? The advanced students.
5. a. the police catch? The thief.
   b. the thief? The police.
6. a. a monster? Tommy.
   b. Tommy dream about? A monster.

PRACTICE 7, p. 148.
2. a. Who did the doctor examine?
   b. Who examined the patient?
3. a. Who called the supervisor?
   b. Who did Miriam call?
4. a. Who surprised the teacher?
   b. Who did the students surprise?
5. a. Who did Andrew and Catherine wait for?
   b. Who waited for Mrs. Allen?

PRACTICE 8, p. 149.
3. Who had a graduation party?
4. Who did Professor Brown invite?
5. Who had a New Year's party?
6. Who did Dr. Martin invite?

PRACTICE 9, p. 149.
2. Who did you talk to?
3. Who did you visit?
4. Who answered the question?
5. Who taught the English class?
6. Who helped you?
7. Who did you help?
8. Who carried the suitcases?
9. Who called?

PRACTICE 10, p. 150.
Present forms:
2. gives (he or she)
3. understand
4. hurt
5. spend
6. shut
7. lend
8. cut
9. hit
10. make
11. cost

PRACTICE 11, p. 150.

2. forgot
3. made
4. gave
5. understood
6. cut, hurt
7. cost
8. spent
9. gave, lent
10. hit, hurt
11. hurt

PRACTICE 12, p. 151.

2. feel
3. keep
4. swim
5. throw
6. draw
7. grow
8. fall
9. win
10. blow

PRACTICE 13, p. 152.

2. drew
3. fell
4. felt
5. threw
6. grew
7. kept
8. swam
9. knew
10. won

PRACTICE 14, p. 153.

Present forms:
2. bend
3. shake
4. become
5. feed
6. bite
7. hide
8. fight
9. build

PRACTICE 15, p. 154.

2. shook
3. fed
4. hid
5. bit, held, shook
6. became
7. fought
8. held
9. bent, bit

PRACTICE 16, p. 154.

Incomplete:
after they left
after several minutes
before school starts
after we finish dinner
Complete:
They left.
Before school starts, I help the teacher.
We ate at a restaurant.
We were at home.

PRACTICE 17, p. 155.

2. 2, 1
   After I looked in the freezer, I closed the freezer door.
   I closed the freezer door after I looked in the freezer.
3. 1, 2
   After I stood on the scale, the nurse wrote down my weight.
   The nurse wrote down my weight after I stood on the scale.
4. 2, 1
   After I put on my exercise clothes, I exercised.
   I exercised after I put on my exercise clothes.
5. 1, 2
   After the alarm rang at the fire station, the firefighters got in their truck.
   The firefighters got in their truck after the alarm rang at the fire station.

PRACTICE 18, p. 156.

2. 2, 1
   b, c
3. 2, 1
   a, d
4. 1, 2
   b, c

PRACTICE 19, p. 157.

2. a. When did the movie start?
   b. When the movie started,
3. a. When you were in high school,
   b. When were you in high school?
4. a. When it snowed,
   b. When did it snow?
5. a. When was Dave sick?
   b. When Dave was sick,

PRACTICE 20, p. 157.

3. When did you hear the good news?
4. When Mr. King died, we felt sad.
5. When were you here?
6. When did we meet?
7. When you arrived, we were happy to see you.
8. When Kevin was absent, the class had a test.
9. When the TV show ended, everyone clapped.
10. When was Mrs. Allen a teacher?

PRACTICE 21, p. 158.

2. a. When did you get sick?
   b. When you got sick, . . . (answers will vary)
3. a. When did the problem begin?
   b. When the problem began, . . .
4. a. When did they visit?
   b. When they visited, . . .

PRACTICE 22, p. 158.

2. were studying.
3. was studying.
4. was studying.
5. were studying.
6. were studying.
7. were not studying.
8. were not studying.
9. was not studying.
10. were not studying.
11. were not studying.
12. was not studying.

PRACTICE 23, p. 159.

3. are sitting
4. were sitting
5. is sitting
6. was sitting
7. are sitting
8. were sitting
9. is sitting
10. was sitting
11. are sitting
12. were sitting

PRACTICE 24, p. 159.

2. a. While I was talking to the teacher yesterday, another student interrupted me.
   b. Another student interrupted me while I was talking to the teacher yesterday.

3. a. A police officer stopped another driver for speeding while we were driving to work.
   b. While we were driving to work, a police officer stopped another driver for speeding.
4. a. While I was walking in the forest, a dead tree fell over.
   b. A dead tree fell over while I was walking in the forest.
5. a. While I was planting flowers in the garden, my dog began to bark at a squirrel.
      My dog began to bark at a squirrel while I was planting flowers in the garden.

PRACTICE 25, p. 160.
2. rang
3. didn't answer
4. wanted
5. noticed
6. was slowing
7. drove
8. saw

PRACTICE 26, p. 161.
2. were sitting
3. came
4. screamed
5. did your cousin do
6. yelled
7. Did your husband do
8. ran
9. was running
10. ran
11. began

PRACTICE 27, p. 161.
1. got
2. called . . . was taking
3. was eating . . . remembered
4. began . . . became
5. was driving . . . saw
6. was exercising . . . came
7. sent . . . was talking . . . told
8. heard . . . stopped

PRACTICE 28, p. 162.
1. a man sat down next to her. OR a man asked her about it.
2. he interrupted her. OR she tried to answer quickly.
3. he continued to talk.
4. he began to tell her about his health. OR he told her about his health.
5. she stood up. OR she excused herself.
6. he was talking to another passenger.

PRACTICE 29, p. 162.
2. When did Simone go to a conference?
3. Who went to a conference last month?
4. Who did you see?
5. Where did you see Ali?

6. What time/When did you see Ali?
7. What is the teacher talking about?
8. Why did the kids play in the pool?
9. Who called?
10. When did they call?
11. Who did you talk to?
12. Where were you last night?
13. What does ancient mean?
14. Where do you live?
15. What does Annie have in her pocket?

PRACTICE 30, p. 163.
Answers will vary.

PRACTICE 31, p. 164.
2. She caught a cold yesterday.
3. She found it on the teacher's desk.
4. Someone stole his wallet.
5. He ate too much for lunch.
6. It sold in three days.
7. It tore when she played outside.
8. She hung up after midnight.
9. Sam bent over and picked it up for her.
10. I caught a taxi.
11. Several students came to class without their homework.
12. I grew up there.

PRACTICE 32, p. 165.
2. broke
3. told
4. spent
5. made
6. wore
7. cost
8. knew
9. met
10. fell
11. lost
12. stole

PRACTICE 33, p. 166.
2. sang
3. flew
4. left
5. won
6. shook
7. built
8. put
9. fought
10. fed

PRACTICE 34, p. 167.
Part I.
1. was
2. saw
3. are
4. am doing
5. Would you like
6. sit
7. need
8. don't need (*Note: non-contracted forms are also correct.*)
9. are you doing
10. am getting
11. is
12. don't trust
13. do you want
14. want
15. had

Part II.

16. saw
17. love
18. stopped
19. reached
20. came
21. was
22. don't believe
23. don't believe
24. are

25. aren't
26. was it
27. did the bee sting
28. are you doing
29. are you holding
30. am holding
31. tricked
32. happened

Part III.

33. got
34. wanted
35. to catch
36. caught
37. looks
38. don't believe
39. is
40. is coming
41. don't see

42. dropped
43. fooled
44. tricked
45. taught
46. learned
47. am
48. have
49. Would you like

CHAPTER 10

PRACTICE 1, p. 170.

2. are going to be
3. is going to be
4. are going to be
5. are going to be
6. are going to be
7. is going to be
8. are going to be
9. is going to be
10. are going to be

PRACTICE 2, p. 170.

1. B: am going to be
2. A: Is Albert going to fix
   B: am going to call
3. A: Are you going to apply
   B: am going to complete
4. A: Are Ed and Nancy going to join
   B: are going to meet

PRACTICE 3, p. 171.

She **is going to wake** up at 5:00. She **is going to have** a quick breakfast of toast and coffee. She **is going to catch** the 5:45 train to work. At 6:30, she **is going to have** a weekly meeting with her employees. For the rest of the morning, she **is going to be** at her desk. She **is going to answer** phone calls and emails, and she **is going to work** on project details. She **is going to answer** a lot of questions. She **is going to have** a big lunch at 11:00. In the afternoon, she **is going to visit** job sites. She **is going to meet** with builders and architects. She **is going to finish** by 7:00 and **is going to be** home by 8:00.

PRACTICE 4, p. 171.

2. am going to eat a big lunch.
3. am going to take some medicine.
4. am going to call the neighbors.
5. is going to do a search on the Internet.
6. are going to look for a bigger place.
7. is going to check the lost-and-found.
8. am going to take it back to the store.

PRACTICE 6, p. 173.

2. You are not going to eat. — Are you going to eat?
3. He is not going to eat. — Is he going to eat?
4. She is not going to eat. — Is she going to eat?
5. We are not going to eat. — Are we going to eat?
6. They are not going to eat. — Are they going to eat?
7. My friend is not going to eat. — Is my friend going to eat?
8. The students are not going to eat. — Are the students going to eat?

PRACTICE 7, p. 173.

1. B: are going to go
   A: Are you going to stay
   B: are going to come
2. A: is Sally going to work
   B: is not going to work . . . is going to take
3. A: Are the students going to have
   B: are going to have
4. A: Are Joan and Bob going to move
   B: is going to start
   A: Are they going to look for
   B: are not going to look for . . . are going to rent

PRACTICE 8, p. 174.

2. They are taking their teenage grandchildren with them.
3. They are staying in parks and campgrounds.
4. They are leaving from Vancouver in June.
5. They are arriving in Montreal in August.
6. Mr. and Mrs. Johnson are driving back home alone.
7. Their grandchildren are flying home because they don't want to miss the beginning of school.
8. Their parents are meeting them at the airport.

PRACTICE 9, p. 175.

2. F
3. P
4. F
5. P
6. F
7. P . . . P
8. F

PRACTICE 10, p. 175.

1. b. last
   c. last
   d. last
   e. yesterday
   f. ago
   g. last
   h. ago
   i. last
   j. yesterday

2. b. next
   c. next
   d. next
   e. tomorrow
   f. in
   g. next
   h. in
   i. tomorrow
   j. tomorrow

PRACTICE 11, p. 176.

2. ago
3. ago
4. last
5. next
6. in
7. yesterday
8. tomorrow
9. in
10. yesterday
11. last
12. tomorrow
13. ago
14. next

PRACTICE 12, p. 176.
6. a couple of years
9. a couple of weeks

PRACTICE 13, p. 177.
3. a few hours
4. a few days
6. a few years

PRACTICE 14, p. 177.
2. a. Susie married Paul a couple of months ago.
   b. Susie is going to marry Paul in a couple of months.
3. a. Dr. Nelson retired a few years ago.
   b. Dr. Nelson is going to retire in a few years.
4. a. Jack began a new job a couple of days ago.
   b. Jack is going to begin a new job in a couple of days.

PRACTICE 15, p. 178.
2. past
3. present
4. past
5. future
6. present
7. present
8. past
9. future
10. past
11. future

PRACTICE 16, p. 178.
2. this morning/today/right now
3. this morning/today
4. this morning/today
5. this morning/today/right now
6. this morning/today

PRACTICE 17, p. 179.
1. b. She overslept. OR She missed her math class.
2. a. She is going to sit in the kitchen.
   b. She is going to think about a solution.
3. She is sitting in her kitchen. OR She is thinking about going to school.

PRACTICE 18, p. 179.
2. will be
3. will be
4. will be
5. will be
6. will be
7. will be
8. will be
9. will be
10. will be

PRACTICE 21, p. 181.
2. You will need extra chairs for the party.
3. Hurry or we won't be on time for the movie.
4. Your brother and sister will help you with your science project.
5. The bus won't be on time today.
6. Watch out! You will cut yourself with that sharp knife.
7. Carlos and Olivia will graduate from nursing school with high grades.

PRACTICE 22, p. 181.
2. Will your friends live to be 100 years old?
3. Will your children live to be 100 years old?
4. Will we live on another planet?
5. Will my friends live on another planet?

6. Will some people live underwater?
7. Will I live underwater?
8. Will countries find a solution for poverty?

PRACTICE 23, p. 182.
2. are going to go   will go
3. are going to go   will go
4. is going to go   will go
5. are going to go   will go
6. is not going to go   will not go
7. am not going to go   will not go
8. are not going to go   will not go
9. Is she going to go   Will she go
10. Are they going to go   Will they go
11. Are you going to go   Will you go

PRACTICE 24, p. 183.
2. Will you need help tomorrow?
3. Did you need help yesterday?
4. Did Eva need help yesterday?
5. Will Eva need help tomorrow?
6. Does Eva need help now?
7. Do the students need help now?
8. Will the students need help tomorrow?
9. Did the students need help yesterday?

PRACTICE 25, p. 183.
2. eats
3. eats
4. has
5. cooked
6. was . . . loved
7. dropped . . . was . . . didn't burn
8. is going to invite (*be going to* = plan)
9. Is she going to cook/Will she cook
10. Is she going to make
11. isn't going to prepare/won't prepare
12. is going to surprise/will surprise

PRACTICE 26, p. 184.
2. Are you going to be/Will you be sick tomorrow?
3. Were you sick yesterday?
4. Was Steve sick yesterday?
5. Is Steve going to be/Will Steve be sick tomorrow?
6. Is Steve sick now?
7. Are your kids sick now?
8. Are your kids going to be/Will your kids be sick tomorrow?
9. Were your kids sick yesterday?

PRACTICE 27, p. 185.
1. am . . . will be/am going to be . . . was . . . will be/am going to be
2. A: were you . . . Were you
   B: wasn't . . . was
   A: was . . . were you
   B: were
   A: was
3. A: Is the post office
   B: isn't . . . is
   A: Are
   B: aren't . . . are

PRACTICE 28, p. 185.
2. Are
3. Do
4. Do
5. Are
6. Do
7. Do
8. Are
9. Do

PRACTICE 29, p. 186.
2. Did
3. Were
4. Were
5. Did
6. Did
7. Did
8. Were

PRACTICE 30, p. 186.

	Every day/Now	Yesterday	Tomorrow
1.	drink am drinking	drank	am going to drink will drink
2.	work are working	worked	are going to work will work
3.	is is	was	is going to be will be
4.	help are helping	helped	are going to help will help
5.	doesn't come isn't coming	didn't come	isn't going to come won't come
6.	doesn't do isn't doing	didn't do	isn't going to do won't do
7.	Do they exercise Are they exercising	Did they exercise	Are they going to exercise Will they exercise
8.	Is he Is he	Was he	Is he going to be Will he be
9.	isn't isn't	wasn't	isn't going to be won't be

PRACTICE 31, p. 187.
1. left
2. A: are you going to wear
   B: am going to wear . . . will be/is going to be
3. A: Did she tell . . . did she tell
   B: told
4. I am making . . . is getting
5. A: Are you going to study
   B: don't have
   B: gave . . . is giving
6. A: Are you going to be/Will you be
   B: is going to have
   B: broke . . . didn't heal
7. A: said
   B: didn't understand
8. A: is
   B: is meeting
9. had . . . ran . . . slammed . . . missed
10. A: Are you going to call
    B: forget

PRACTICE 32, p. 189.
1. lived
2. were
3. didn't have
4. decided
5. took
6. met
7. will buy
8. will give
9. took
10. was
11. are
12. don't have
13. threw
14. saw
15. climbed
16. found
17. will eat
18. Are you going to give
19. is
20. fell
21. was
22. didn't want
23. went
24. never caught
25. ran
26. died
27. lived

CHAPTER 11

PRACTICE 1, p. 190.
2. sure
3. sure
4. unsure
5. unsure
6. sure
7. unsure
8. unsure
9. sure

PRACTICE 3, p. 191.
2. a. You might need to see a doctor soon.
   b. Maybe you will need to see a doctor soon.
3. a. We may play basketball after school.
   b. We might play basketball after school.
4. a. Maybe our class will go to a movie together.
   b. Our class may go to a movie together.

PRACTICE 4, p. 191.
2. a
3. b
4. a
5. b
6. a, b
7. b

PRACTICE 5, p. 192.
2. They may come.   They might come.
3. She might not study.   She may not study.
4. We might not need help. We may not need help.
5. I might not need help. I may not need help
6. He may understand.   Maybe he will understand.
7. You may understand.   Maybe you will understand.
8. They may understand.   Maybe they will understand.

PRACTICE 6, p. 192.
2. It may snow next week./It might snow next week./
   Maybe it will snow next week.
3. We may go ice-skating on the lake./We might go ice-
   skating on the lake./Maybe we will go ice-skating on
   the lake.
4. The kids will play in the snow.
5. The snow won't melt for several days.

PRACTICE 7, p. 193.
2. a, b, d
3. a, b, c
4. b, d

PRACTICE 8, p. 193.
2. 2, 1
   a. Before I turn in my homework, I am going to
      check my answers.
   b. After I check my answers, I am going to turn in
      my homework.

3. 2, 1
   a. After I clear off the table, I am going to wash the dishes.
   b. Before I wash the dishes, I am going to clear off the table.
4. 1, 2
   a. After I get my umbrella, I am going to go out in the rain.
   Before I go out in the rain, I am going to get my umbrella.
5. 2, 1
   a. After I go to the departure gate, I am going to board the airplane.
   b. Before I board the airplane, I am going to go to the departure gate.

PRACTICE 9, p. 194.
2. he goes to school, he is going to eat breakfast.
3. he gets to school, he is going to go to his classroom.
4. he has lunch in the cafeteria, he is going to talk to his friends.
5. he cooks dinner for his roommates, he is going to pick up food at the grocery store.
6. he goes to bed, he is going to do his homework.
7. he falls asleep, he is going to have good dreams.

PRACTICE 10, p. 195.
2. have . . . am going to go
3. see . . . are going to make
4. takes . . . is going to practice
5. takes . . . is going to feel
6. gets . . . is going to be

PRACTICE 11, p. 195.
2. goes . . . is going to study
3. enjoys . . . will take
4. will apply . . . does
5. attends . . . is going to study
6. completes . . . is going to work

PRACTICE 12, p. 196.
2. rains . . . am not going to/will not spend
3. gets . . . are going to/will be
4. are going to/will get . . . does not do
5. gets . . . is going to/will earn
6. doesn't get . . . is going to/will delay
7. feels . . . is not going to/will not come
8. is going to/will call . . . misses
9. needs . . . are going to/will help
10. are going to/will make . . . does not need

PRACTICE 13, p. 196.
3. talks
4. is going to/will meet
5. agree
6. is going to/will buy
7. says
8. is going to/will surprise
9. does not say
10. is going to/will save

PRACTICE 14, p. 197.
2. Will he get to work on time? Yes, he will.
3. Will he stay awake at work? Yes, he will.
4. Will he delete emails before he reads them? No, he won't.
5. Will he answer his phone? Yes, he will.
6. Will he help his co-workers when they ask? Yes, he will?
7. Will he tell his co-workers he is too busy? No, he won't.
8. Will his father and co-workers be happy? Yes, they will.

PRACTICE 15, p. 198.
Part I.
2. a
3. e
4. c
5. b
6. g
7. d
Part II.
2. If I cry, my eyes get red.
3. If I don't pay my electric bill, I have no electricity.
4. If the phone rings in the middle of the night, I don't answer it.
5. If I get to work late, I stay at work late.
6. If I have a big breakfast, I have a lot of energy.
7. If I don't do my homework, I get low grades on the tests.

PRACTICE 17, p. 199.
2. future
3. future
4. present habit
5. present habit
6. future
7. future
8. present habit
9. future

PRACTICE 18, p. 200.
2. are going to go . . . is
3. go . . . am going to meet
4. go . . . usually meet
5. am going to buy . . . go
6. is . . . gets . . . feels . . . exercises . . . exercises . . . begins
7. am . . . am not going to exercise
8. travels . . . brings
9. travels . . . is going to pack
10. is . . . begins
11. gets . . . is going to tell

PRACTICE 19, p. 201.
2. What did they do
3. What are they going to do
4. What will they do
5. What do they do
6. What is he doing
7. What did you (we) do
8. What is she going to do
9. What are you going to do
10. What do you do
11. What does he do

PRACTICE 20, p. 202.
2. What do you do?
3. What do you (we) do?
4. What do they do?
5. What does she do?
6. What do they do?
7. What do I do?

PRACTICE 21, p. 202.
2. c
3. c
4. a
5. d
6. a
7. c
8. c

PRACTICE 22, p. 203.
1. A: Are you going to stay
   B: am going to take . . . am going to visit
   A: are you going to be
2. A: isn't . . . left
   A: Is she going to be
   A: did she go
   B: went
3. A: are you wearing
   B: broke
   B: stepped
4. A: Are you going to see
   B: am not going to have
   A: Are you going to see
   A: borrowed . . . forgot

PRACTICE 23, p. 204.
1. are
2. are staying
3. like
4. always makes
5. tells
6. go
7. went
8. asked
9. agreed
10. put
11. brushed
12. sat
13. are you going to tell
14. begin
15. am going to give
16. love
17. am going to tell
18. was
19. was
20. saw
21. was
22. ran
23. stayed
24. was
25. got
26. stayed
27. found
28. needed
29. to eat
30. put
31. didn't smell
32. didn't see
33. hopped
34. found
35. saw
36. looked
37. heard
38. didn't see
39. decided
40. wanted
41. to rest
42. said
43. heard
44. spotted
45. flew
46. picked
47. didn't know
48. ate
49. are
50. expect
51. Do you understand
52. have
53. am going to go
54. to get
55. is/is going to be
56. are we going to do
57. have
58. are going to go
59. are
60. are going to see
61. are going to see
62. see
63. are going to have
64. are going to have

CHAPTER 12

PRACTICE 1, p. 208.
2. can speak
3. can speak
4. can speak
5. can speak
6. can speak
7. can speak
8. can speak
9. can speak
10. can speak
11. can speak

PRACTICE 2, p. 208.
2. can't
3. can't
4. can
5. can
6. can

PRACTICE 4, p. 209.
2. Can George and Eva play the piano? Yes, they can.
3. Can George drive a car? Yes, he can.
4. Can Paul play the piano? Yes, he can.
5. Can Mia, George, and Paul swim? Yes, they can.
6. Can Paul and Eva drive a car? No, they can't.
7. Can Eva and George repair a bike? No, they can't.
8. Can Eva, Paul, and George play the piano? Yes, they can.

PRACTICE 5, p. 210.
2. Can you do work processing? Yes, I can.
3. Can you speak English? No, I can't.
4. Can you lift suitcases? No, I can't.
5. Can you work weekends? Yes, I can.

PRACTICE 6, p. 210.
1. e
2. c
3. b
4. a
5. d

PRACTICE 7, p. 210.
2. Martha knows how to play chess.
3. Sonya and Thomas know how to speak Portuguese.
4. Jack doesn't know how to speak Russian.
5. My brothers don't know how to cook.
6. I don't know how to change a flat tire.
7. We don't know how to play musical instruments.
8. Do you know how to type?
9. Do your children know how to swim?
10. Does Ari know how to kick a soccer ball very far?

PRACTICE 9, p. 212.
2. They could cook over a fire.
3. They could read books.
4. They could spend time together.
5. They couldn't use a computer.
6. They couldn't turn on the lights.
7. They couldn't use electric heat.
8. They could have heat from a fireplace.
9. They could play board games.

PRACTICE 10, p. 213.
1. couldn't
2. can't
3. Could
4. can
5. could
6. Could
7. can't

PRACTICE 11, p. 213.
2. he couldn't go swimming.
   he can go swimming.
3. he couldn't play soccer.
   he can play soccer.
4. he couldn't ride a bike.
   he can ride a bike.

PRACTICE 13, p. 214.
2. You are able to draw. You were able to draw. You will be able to draw.
3. He is able to drive. He was able to drive. He will be able to drive.
4. She is able to swim. She was able to swim. She will be able to swim.
5. We are able to dance. We were able to dance. We will be able to dance.
6. They are able to type. They were able to type. They will be able to type.

PRACTICE 15, p. 214.
2. a
3. b
4. c
5. c

PRACTICE 16, p. 215.
2. wasn't able to ask
3. weren't able to give
4. wasn't able to visit
5. wasn't able to have
6. was able to understand
7. were able to have
8. was able to learn
9. was able to visit

PRACTICE 17, p. 216.
1. b, e
2. a, b, e
3. a, b
4. e
5. b

PRACTICE 18, p. 216.
2. very
3. very
4. too
5. too
6. very
7. very
8. too

PRACTICE 19, p. 217.
2. a
3. b
4. b
5. a
6. a
7. b
8. a

PRACTICE 21, p. 218.
1. b
2. c
3. d
4. a
5. d
6. a
7. d

PRACTICE 22, p. 218.
1. was
2. hunted
3. took
4. listened
5. dreamed/dreamt
6. decided
7. are you leaving
8. are you going
9. am going
10. am going
11. do you want
12. to go
13. want
14. to experience
15. need
16. to learn
17. can learn
18. stay
19. can't stay
20. is
21. will have★
22. get
23. will face
24. may never see
25. will try
26. Do you need
27. can I cross
28. don't know
29. can't cross
30. won't be able
31. will help
32. will give
33. can jump
34. will also give
35. don't lose
36. will reach
37. are you lying
38. Are you
39. can't see
40. drank
41. am
42. will die
43. can't find
44. gave
45. can I give
46. will give
47. can see
48. can't see
49. will you find
50. will carry
51. can't go
52. will I do
53. have
54. will find
55. can't see
56. can hear
57. can't help
58. am dying
59. are you dying
60. lost
61. can't find
62. am starving/will starve
63. can help
64. will give
65. can smell
66. can I help
67. am trying
68. need
69. to go
70. will put
71. (will) take
72. couldn't see
73. couldn't smell
74. lost
75. heard
76. aren't
77. never lost
78. am flying

★*be going to* is also possible for the *will* answers.

CHAPTER 13

PRACTICE 1, p. 223.
2. should study
3. should study
4. should study
5. should study
6. should study
7. should study
8. should study
9. should study

PRACTICE 2, p. 223.
2. should
3. shouldn't
4. shouldn't
5. should
6. should
7. shouldn't

PRACTICE 3, p. 224.
3. She should study for her tests.
4. She shouldn't stay up late.
5. She shouldn't daydream in class.
6. She shouldn't be absent from class a lot.
7. She should take notes during lectures.
8. She should take her books to school.

PRACTICE 4, p. 224.
Sample answers:
2. should talk to the Browns.
3. should rest.
4. should call the dentist.
5. should save his money.
6. should get visas.

PRACTICE 5, p. 225.
2. have to leave
3. have to leave
4. have to leave
5. has to leave
6. has to leave
7. don't have to leave
8. don't have to leave
9. doesn't have to leave
10. don't have to leave

PRACTICE 6, p. 225.
3. has to
4. doesn't have to
5. doesn't have to
6. has to
7. has to

PRACTICE 7, p. 226.
2. don't have to
3. has to
4. have to
5. don't have to
6. have to
7. doesn't have to
8. have to
9. has to
10. doesn't have to

PRACTICE 8, p. 226.
2. had to
3. didn't have to
4. had to
5. didn't have to
6. had to
7. didn't have to
8. had to

PRACTICE 9, p. 227.
2. didn't have to
3. didn't have to
4. had to
5. didn't have to
6. had to
7. didn't have to
8. had to

PRACTICE 11, p. 228.
2. must
3. must not
4. must
5. must not
6. must not

PRACTICE 12, p. 228.
2. must not
3. must
4. must not
5. must
6. must

PRACTICE 13, p. 229.
2. should
3. must
4. should
5. must
6. should
7. should
8. must
9. must

PRACTICE 14, p. 229.
Sample answers:
2. May/Could/Can I look at your dictionary for a minute?
3. May/Could/Can I please sharpen my pencil?
4. May/Could/Can I please borrow your cell phone?
5. May/Could/Can I please get a new library card?

PRACTICE 15, p. 230.
Sample answers:
2. Could/Would you please clean your bedroom?
3. Could/Would you please give me some money for a movie?
4. Could/Would you please turn down the TV?
5. Could/Would you please bring me some fresh cream?
6. Could/Would you please take a picture of us?

PRACTICE 16, p. 230.
1. a, b
2. b, c
3. a, c

PRACTICE 17, p. 231.
2. STUDENT: Do we have any homework for tomorrow?
   TEACHER: Yes. <u>Read</u> pages 24 through 36, and <u>answer</u> the questions on page 37, in writing.
   STUDENT: Is that all?
   TEACHER: Yes.
3. HEIDI: Please <u>close</u> the window, Mike. It's a little chilly in here.
   MIKE: Okay. Is there anything else I can do for you before I leave?
   HEIDI: Could you turn off the light in the kitchen?
   MIKE: No problem. Anything else?
   HEIDI: Umm, please <u>hand</u> me the remote control for the TV. It's over there.
   MIKE: Sure. Here.
   HEIDI: Thanks.
   MIKE: I'll stop by again tomorrow. <u>Take</u> care of yourself. <u>Take</u> good care of that broken leg.
   HEIDI: <u>Don't worry</u>. I will. Thanks again

PRACTICE 18, p. 231.
Answers may vary:
1. Put some oil in a pan.
2. Heat the oil.
3. Put the popcorn in the pan.

4. Cover the pan with a lid.
5. Shake the pan.
6. Stop shaking the pan when the popcorn stops popping.
7. Pour the popcorn into a bowl.
8. Pour melted butter over the popcorn.
9. Salt the popcorn.
10. Enjoy your snack!

PRACTICE 19, p. 232.
3. Don't talk
4. Do
5. Don't copy
6. Work
7. Answer

PRACTICE 20, p. 232.
3. Follow
4. Turn off
5. Don't play
6. Use
7. Talk
8. Ask
9. Don't download

PRACTICE 21, p. 233.
2. Ø
3. Ø
4. to
5. Ø
6. Ø
7. to
8. Ø
9. to
10. Ø

PRACTICE 22, p. 233.
2. a
3. b
4. c
5. c
6. c
7. a
8. b

PRACTICE 23, p. 234.
Sample answers:
2. Let's relax.
3. Let's have a party for her.
4. Let's eat.
5. Let's go there for dinner.

PRACTICE 24, p. 235.
2. c
3. c
4. a
5. b
6. a
7. c
8. b
9. c
10. a

PRACTICE 25, p. 235.
1. a, c
2. c
3. b, d
4. b, d
5. b, d
6. a, b, d
7. b, d

CHAPTER 14

PRACTICE 1, p. 237.

Adjectives	*Nouns*
tall	clothes
pretty	pens
sad	boat
hot	store
true	horse
happy	truth

PRACTICE 2, p. 237.
1. delicious, old, chicken, tasty
2. camera, old, cell
3. old, English, sad, grammar

PRACTICE 3, p. 238.
2. noun
3. noun
4. adjective
5. adjective
6. noun
7. noun
8. adjective

PRACTICE 4, p. 238.
Adjective + Noun
2. dangerous, old, noisy, smelly apartment
3. old, smelly sandwich
4. old, smelly shirt
Noun + Noun
2. apartment stairs
3. sandwich recipe
4. shirt sleeves

PRACTICE 5, p. 238.
2. magazine article
3. business card
4. dentist appointment
5. chicken salad
6. house key
7. computer cord
8. milk carton
9. clothes store
10. shower curtain

PRACTICE 6, p. 239.
2. a. messy kitchen
   b. kitchen cabinets
   c. kitchen counter
3. a. city bus
   b. bus schedule
   c. bus route
4. a. airplane noise
   b. airplane movie
   c. airplane ticket
5. a. apartment manager
   b. one-bedroom apartment
   c. apartment building
6. a. phone number
   b. broken phone
   c. phone call

7. a. hospital patient
   b. sick patient
   c. patient information

PRACTICE 7, p. 240.
2. spicy Mexican food
3. kind young man
4. dirty brown glass
5. lovely tall rose bush
6. interesting small old paintings
7. important new foreign film
8. little yellow flowers
9. tall middle-aged woman
10. antique Chinese wooden cabinet

Exercise 8, p. 241.
2. b   6. a
3. b   7. b
4. b   8. a
5. a   9. a

PRACTICE 9, p. 242.
2. sound
5. taste
6. smell
7. look
9. felt
10. seems

PRACTICE 10, p. 242.
Sample answers: 5. terrible
2. tired   6. bad
3. good   7. fun
4. great   8. terrible

PRACTICE 11, p. 243.
2. clearly   9. quickly
3. neatly   10. slowly
4. correctly   11. late
5. hard   12. honestly
6. well   13. fast
7. early   14. easily
8. carefully

PRACTICE 12, p. 243.
2. easily   7. well
3. late   8. honestly
4. safely   9. softly
5. fast   10. carelessly
6. hard

PRACTICE 13, p. 244.
2. beautifully . . . beautiful . . . beautiful
3. good . . . well
4. good . . . good
5. interesting . . . interesting
6. bad . . . bad
7. fast . . . fast

PRACTICE 14, p. 244.
2. correctly . . . correct
3. late . . . late
4. beautiful . . . beautifully

5. honest . . . honestly
6. handsome . . . handsome
7. good . . . good
8. easily . . . easy
9. well . . . good
10. quickly . . . quick
11. sweet . . . sweet
12. careless . . . carelessly

PRACTICE 15, p. 245.
2. slowly   7. fluent . . . fluently
3. hard   8. neat
4. hard   9. carefully
5. clear   10. good
6. early   11. well

PRACTICE 16, p. 246.
2. c
3. b . . . a
4. a

PRACTICE 17, p. 246.
2. 90%   7. 30%
3. 100%   8. 88%
4. 60%   9. 100%
5. 50%   10. 97%
6. 75%

PRACTICE 18, p. 246.
2. are   7. are
3. is   8. is
4. is   9. is
5. are   10. are
6. are

PRACTICE 19, p. 247.
2. are   10. is
3. is   11. are
4. are   12. is
5. is   13. is
6. are   14. are
7. are   15. is
8. is   16. are
9. are

PRACTICE 20, p. 247.
1. c   5. b
2. a   6. c
3. b   7. a
4. b

PRACTICE 21, p. 248.
2. a   6. b
3. b   7. a
4. b   8. b
5. a

PRACTICE 22, p. 248.
2. a   7. a
3. b   8. b
4. a   9. a
5. a   10. a
6. b

PRACTICE 23, p. 249.
2. Every **student** is . . .
4. . . . sink **is** dirty.
5. Where **do** all . . .
7. . . . family like**s**
8. **Does** everyone . . .
10. **Were** all . . .
11. . . . Everyone **is** . . .

PRACTICE 24, p. 250.
1. anything
2. someone/somebody
3. something/anything
4. someone/somebody/anyone/anybody
5. something . . . anything
6. someone/somebody . . . anyone/anybody
7. something/anything
8. someone/somebody/anyone/anybody

PRACTICE 25, p. 250.
1. a, c, d, e
2. a, b, c, d, e, f
3. a, c, f
4. b, f

PRACTICE 26, p. 251.
2. anyone/anybody
3. something
4. someone/somebody
5. anything/something
6. anyone/anybody/someone/somebody
7. A: something
   B: anything
8. A: anything/something
   B: anything
9. A: someone/somebody . . . someone/somebody/
      anyone/anybody
   B: anyone/anybody
10. A: anyone/anybody
    B: Someone/Somebody
11. A: something/anything
    B: anything
12. A: someone/somebody (OR: something = possibly an
       animal)
    B: anyone/anything
    A: anyone . . . anything

CHAPTER 15

PRACTICE 1, p. 252.
2. wider than
3. cheaper than
4. darker than
5. smarter than
6. older than
7. happier than
8. more important than
9. more difficult than
10. more expensive than
11. easier than
12. funnier than
13. better than
14. farther/further than
15. fatter than

16. hotter than
17. thinner than
18. worse than
19. prettier than
20. more famous than

PRACTICE 2, p. 253.
2. funnier than
3. more interesting than
4. smarter than
5. wider than
6. larger than
7. darker than
8. better than
9. worse than
10. more confusing than
11. farther/further . . . than
12. better than
13. easier than
14. more beautiful than

PRACTICE 3, p. 253.
Sample answers:
2. Life in the city is more expensive than life in the
   country.
3. Life in the suburbs is more relaxing than life in the city.
4. Life in the city is busier than life in the country.
5. Life in the suburbs is more convenient than life in the
   country.
6. Life in the country is more beautiful than life in the
   suburbs.
7. Life in the country is cheaper than life in the city.
8. Life in the country is nicer than life in the city.
9. Life in the suburbs is safer than life in the city.
10. Life in the country is better than life in the city.

PRACTICE 4, p. 254.
2. 101B is more boring than 101A.
3. 101B is harder than 101A.
4. 101A is easier than 101B.
5. 101A is more popular than 101B.
6. 101B is more difficult than 101A.
7. 101A is more enjoyable than 101B.

PRACTICE 5, p. 255.
2. lazier than . . . the laziest
3. cleaner than . . . the cleanest
4. older than . . . the oldest
5. younger than . . . the youngest
6. newer than . . . the newest
7. more beautiful than . . . the most beautiful
8. more exciting than . . . the most exciting
9. nicer than . . . the nicest
10. quieter than . . . the quietest
11. worse than . . . the worst
12. fatter than . . . the fattest
13. thinner than . . . the thinnest
14. hotter than . . . the hottest
15. better than . . . the best
16. cheaper than . . . the cheapest
17. farther/further than . . . the farthest/the furthest

PRACTICE 6, p. 256.
2. The most beautiful city in the world is . . .
3. The most interesting show on TV is . . .

4. The most boring sport to watch is . . .
5. The easiest language to learn is . . .
6. The most talented movie star is . . .
7. The most relaxing place to go for vacation is . . .
8. The best place to live is . . .

PRACTICE 7, p. 256.
Sample answers:
1. A 5-star restaurant is the most expensive.
2. A fast-food restaurant is the most convenient.
3. A 5-star restaurant is the most relaxing.
4. A fast-food restaurant is the busiest.
5. A 5-star restaurant is the nicest.
6. An Internet café is the most interesting.
7. A fast-food restaurant is the most popular.
8. An Internet café is the quietest.
9. A fast-food restaurant is the cheapest.
10. An Internet café is the most useful.

PRACTICE 8, p. 257.
Sample answers:
2. Rex is the most active.
   Rex is more active than Polly.
3. Fluffy is the youngest.
   Fluffy is younger than Rex.
4. Rex is the heaviest.
   Rex is heavier than Polly.
5. Polly is the most colorful.
   Polly is more colorful than Fluffy.
6. Rex is the biggest.
   Rex is bigger than Polly.
7. Polly is the oldest.
   Polly is older than Fluffy.
8. Polly is the smallest.
   Polly is smaller than Rex.
9. Polly is the lightest.
   Polly is lighter than Rex.

PRACTICE 9, p. 258.
2. the fastest cars
3. the happiest families
4. the funniest children
5. the best managers
6. the tallest women
7. the oldest men
8. the most interesting **people**
9. the scariest animals
10. the easiest languages . . . the hardest languages

PRACTICE 10, p. 259.
2. . . . is one of the most dangerous sports.
3. . . . is one of the most expensive sports.
4. . . . is one of the safest sports.
5. . . . is one of the most difficult sports.
6. . . . is one of the most interesting sports.
7. . . . is one of the best sports for your heart.

PRACTICE 11, p. 259.
2. . . . is one of the biggest cities.
3. . . . is one of the hardest languages to learn.
4. . . . is one of the most interesting places to visit.
5. . . . is one of the prettiest places to visit.
6. . . . is one of the most expensive cities
7. . . . is one of the most important **people**

PRACTICE 12, p. 260.
2. bigger than
3. the hottest places
4. the coldest places
5. longer than
6. larger
7. the largest
8. the longest
9. The smallest
10. scarier than
11. the scariest
12. the most dangerous animal**s**
13. the most expensive cit**ies**
14. more expensive

PRACTICE 13, p. 261.

	Adjective	*Adverb*	*Comparative*	*Superlative*
2.	clear	clearly	more clearly	the most clearly
3.	slow	slowly	more slowly	the most slowly
4.	beautiful	beautifully	more beautifully	the most beautifully
5.	neat	neatly	more neatly	the most neatly
6.	careful	carefully	more carefully	the most carefully
7.	fluent	fluently	more fluently	the most fluently
8.	good	well	better	the best
9.	hard	hard	harder	the hardest
10.	early	early	earlier	the earliest
11.	late	late	later	the latest
12.	fast	fast	faster	the fastest

PRACTICE 14, p. 261.
2. more carefully than
3. the most quickly
4. the hardest
5. later than
6. the earliest
7. better than
8. more quickly than
9. more slowly than
10. the most fluently
11. faster than
12. the best

PRACTICE 15, p. 262.
2. more dangerous than
3. more dangerously than
4. the most dangerously
5. more clearly than
6. clearer than
7. the most clearly
8. harder than
9. the hardest
10. better than
11. the best
12. better than
13. longer than
14. the longest
15. neater than
16. more neatly than

PRACTICE 16, p. 263.
2. as
3. Ø
4. Ø
5. from
6. to
7. Ø
8. Ø

PRACTICE 17, p. 263.
3. similar
4. similar
5. different
6. similar to
7. different from
8. similar to

9. different
10. different from

PRACTICE 18, p. 264.
2. Trains and buses are similar.
   Trains are similar to buses.
3. Your grammar book is the same as my grammar book.
   Your grammar book and my grammar book are the same.
4. Women and men are different.
   Women are different from men.

PRACTICE 19, p. 264.
2. alike	8. like
3. alike	9. alike
4. alike	10. like
5. like	11. alike
6. alike	12. like
7. like	

PRACTICE 20, p. 265.
Sample answers:
2. White chocolate and dark chocolate are alike. They are sweet.
3. Magazines are like newspapers. They have articles.
4. Scissors and knives are alike. They are sharp.
5. Malaysia and Thailand are alike. They are hot.
6. Ice-cream cones are like milkshakes. They are delicious.
7. Chemistry and physics are alike. They are difficult.

PRACTICE 21, p. 265.
1. a, e
2. b, d
3. b (Some people may also say e.)

PRACTICE 22, p. 266.
Checked statements: 2, 3, 5

PRACTICE 23, p. 267.
Sample answers:
2. cold	6. cheap/inexpensive
3. hard	7. comfortable
4. complicated	8. cool
5. short	9. heavy
	10. new

PRACTICE 24, p. 267.
2. can	10. don't
3. do	11. is
4. don't	12. can't
5. doesn't	13. won't
6. wasn't	14. are
7. will	15. was
8. does	16. did
9. didn't	17. aren't

PRACTICE 25, p. 268.
Sample answers:
2. cats don't
3. people can't
4. flowers do
5. the weather in the mountains isn't.
6. loose shoes are
7. lemons aren't
8. was/wasn't . . . is/isn't
9. won't
10. aren't

PRACTICE 26, p. 268.
2. b	8. c
3. c	9. b
4. a	10. a
5. d	11. a
6. b	12. d
7. c	

NOTES